Forensic Linguistics Articles

MW00929823

Forensic Linguistics Articles

Lucian Lupescu

Copyright © 2019 by Lucian Lupescu

All rights reserved. This book or any portion thereof may not be reproduced or used in any manner whatsoever without the express written permission of the publisher except for the use of brief quotations in a book review or scholarly journal.

First Printing: 2019

ISBN 978-0-359-81322-3

Email: L.Lupescu@yahoo.com

Table of Contents

ON THE "LINGUISTIC FINGERPRINT"

Linguists use the term "idiolect" to define an individual's unique use of language (in other words, one's "linguistic fingerprint"), but this term seems to be more of a convention than a scientific, objective fact. At the time of writing there is no general consensus on *one* theory that would explain or definitively prove the existence of an actual "linguistic fingerprint" (for more studies, theories, and approaches see the **Further reading** section). More than that, the American linguist Noam Chomsky claimed even (in his famous Universal Grammar theory) that we cannot explain or predict one's linguistic performance (meaning one's actual expression of language), or the "E-language" (E = external), because this is just a form of one's innate linguistic competence, the "I-language" (I = internal), modified by external stimuli. In this case, a complete understanding of one's performance phenomena is, according to Chomsky, beyond the scope of scientific investigation. In his view, the properties of an E-language are determined by how an I-language is used, and as such their systematic characterization in a theory will be practically impossible (Chomsky 1986, 1988, 1995, 2000; Barber 2014).

Another, more obvious, practical problem in trying to identify the author of a non-genre text is that there is too much variation in a person's use of language (or "style") over the years, depending on that person's experiences, ulterior education, etc. What may also influence that person's writing style at a particular point in time is a person's mood, as well as to whom the text is addressed, or if the text is written in a rush or not, thus spelling, grammar, or punctuation mistakes occurring. Because of the "free" nature of non-genre texts (in the sense that they are not necessarily subjected to the constraints of a genre), they are inherently more chaotic, the writer sometimes mixing registers, changing the meaning of one or more word, or going from one topic to another without any segue. All these variables determine one's style (or one's idiolect) to never be fixed, predictable, or permanent, making it harder for a forensic linguist to clearly pinpoint the true author of a text.

With that being said, there seem to be, however, consistencies in the writing of a particular person at *a particular point in time*, and similarities in regard to the use of language within social groups of any kind (ethnicity, age, gender). The social background of a person influences the way in which he or she uses the language. A sociolinguist can distinguish in a person's linguistic acts such phenomena as diglossia (the use of language in a more "high- standard" manner by the upper class, as opposed to a more "low-standard" use, by the lower class), domain (the use of language is different in different social contexts), register (language used in association with a certain topic, activity, etc.), or analyze them from a pragmatic point of view (the meaning of words in a social context).

There have been observed also several differences between the two genders' use of language (we are talking about *gender*, not *sex*, as they are not always the same). One of those differences is that the feminine gender, supposedly, uses more self-disclosure language in their communication with others than the male gender, presenting a tendency to share their problems, experiences and feelings, to offer or to ask for emotional support. This is in contrast with the masculine gender's supposed tendency toward non-self-disclosure, their use of language emphasizing more a concern to find solutions and offer advice when confronted to a problem (Tannen 1990; Dindia & Allen 1992).

In conclusion, there might not be a "linguistic fingerprint" in the strict sense, as in the real fingerprint that remains the same over the course of one's lifetime, but there are enough consistencies within a social group, it seems, that allow us to reduce the number of authors that could have written a non-genre text. There are also enough consistencies in the writing of a particular person at a particular point in their life that allow us sometimes to be able to say whether they is or is not the author of a particular non-genre text. It seems that if one has to determine the authorship of a text, one must analyze the other texts written by the potential author (or authors) at the time when the text in question was written. This is probably the most reliable way to determine as objectively as possible the real authors of that text (or at least to narrow the field to a few candidates) without any concern that their style might have changed over time.

References:

1. Barber, A. (2014) Idiolects. In *The Stanford Encyclopedia of Philosophy*, Edward N. Zalta (ed.). [Online] Available from: http://plato.stanford.edu/entries/idiolects/

2. Chomsky, N. (1986) *Knowledge of Language: Its Nature, Origin, and Use*, New York: Praeger.

3. Chomsky, N. (1988) *Language and Problems of Knowledge: The Managua Lectures*, Cambridge, Mass.: MIT Press.

4. Chomsky, N. (1995) Language and Nature. In *Mind*, 104 (413): 1-61.

5. Chomsky, N. (2000) *New Horizons in the Study of Language and Mind*, Cambridge, UK: Cambridge University Press.

6. Dindia, K. and Allen, M. (1992) Sex differences in disclosure: A meta-analysis. In *Psychological Bulletin*, 112, 106-124

7. Tannen, D. (1990) *You Just Don't Understand: Women and Men in Conversation.* New York: Harper Collins

Further reading:

1. Coulthard, M. and Johnson, A. (2007) *An introduction to forensic linguistics: language in evidence.* London: Routledge.

2. Coulthard, M. and Johnson, A. (eds.) (2013) *The Routledge Handbook of Forensic Linguistics.* London: Routledge

3. McMenamin, G.R. (2002) *Forensic Linguistics: Advances in Forensic Stylistics.* CRC Press.

4. Olsson, J. and Luchjenbroers, J. (2014). *Forensic linguistics. Third edition.* London: Bloomsbury Academic.

5. Tiersma, P.M. and Solan, L.M. (eds.) (2012) *The Oxford Handbook of Language and Law.* Oxford: Oxford University Press

AGENCY ANALYSIS IN FORENSIC LINGUISTICS

Unlike with the notion of "idiolect", which is easy to define but hard to prove in practice, for the concept of "agency" (also called, according to Michael Bamberg (2005), "agentivity" or "animacy") is easy to find practical examples, but very hard to give a clear definition of what exactly it is. D.A. Cruse (1973) showed that agentivity is understood mostly intuitively and a clear- cut definition is still elusive. Mustafa Emirbayer and Ann Mische (1998) tried to define "human agency" as "the temporally constructed engagement by actors of different structural environments—the temporal-relational contexts of action—which, through the interplay of habit, imagination, and judgment, both reproduces and transforms those structures in interactive response to the problems posed by changing historical situations." This definition can be useful for philosophy, psychology or sociology; however it is still hard to apply it clearly to linguistics, the authors referring to their perspective as "relational pragmatics." Their approach is purely theoretical, and no practical, linguistic examples are given to support this view. It can work for the first aspect of agency given by Bamberg (2005): "agency as an epistemic issue ... central to the study of self, identity, and personhood". However, for the purpose of this essay, Bamberg's (2005) second meaning of agency is more fitting: "the linguistic marking of different perspectives in which represented characters are viewed as relating to objects and to other characters in the (represented) world." In this sense, one can distinguish a number of agentive meta-structures of a text: action, event, situation, response, justification, evaluation, summary. This paper will try to analyze how

10

these basic meta-structures appear in two forensic linguistic cases, as presented by John Olsson in chapters 1 ("The barrel killer") and 12 ("A genocide in Rwanda") from his book, *Wordcrime* (2013).

The case of the "barrel killer" confronts us with a narrator who tries to **deceive** the reader. Howard Simmerson tries to **divert** the investigators' attention away from him; he tries to convince the others that he is not involved by assuming the point of view of the victim. Simmerson knows he is guilty but tries to fool the readers, his intention being to get away with murder. The close examination of the meta-structures used here can show us how he does that. Firstly, he makes it look like Julie Turner performed an **action** (she left). Secondly, Simmerson creates a false **response** from Julie, writing the text messages ("Stopping at jills, back later need to sort my head out," "Tell kids not to worry. sorting my life out. be in touch to get some things," etc.) (Olsson 2013: 6, 7). Thirdly, he creates a false **situation** for Julie, saying to the police that "she was on heavy medication" (Olsson 2013: 8), this providing also a false **justification** for her behavior (the false justification is supported also by the texts sent by Simmerson in Julie's name). In his police interview, Simmerson also **evaluates** Julie's behavior, by implying that it's completely her fault that she disappeared. The letter Simmerson wrote shows that he believed the agent to be external, as if someone else ("God" or "fate") had pushed him to do that, thus not making him directly responsible for his actions: "I love her dearly but I can see it coming to the final shot to finally be together. I am sane writing this and just waiting for the machine to carry this out" (Olsson 2013: 10). The phrasing in these two sentences suggests a sort of fatality, a sort of unavoidable conclusion that can only end in death.

In the second case, the Rwanda genocide, the point of view is very subjective. The statements can be considered unreliable because the witnesses seem to be guided by the interviewer what to say, or they seem to have some bias against the person in question (Mr. U).The witnesses' answers seem to reflect not exactly the real facts, but what they think it happened; they seem to confuse memories of stories they heard with their own memories of facts that actually happened (it is also possible they do that on purpose, to make Mr. U seem more guilty then he actually was). Here, the narrators' speech downplays the role of the suspect, more than that, it makes him even look guilty and morally questionable. Indeed, in this case it is a question of **morals** – the narrators feel they are morally righteous and Mr. U is not. They **don't really want to deceive** the reader; they just feel they are right. The intention is to get the guilty one, no matter what the truth is, ignoring the actual facts. Bamberg's (2005) statement fits here perfectly: "speakers (...) downplay or foreground characters' (as well as their own) involvement in narrated events and event sequences, and also create evaluations and stances with regard to who is morally right or at fault." This case brings up another problem when dealing with text analysis (emphasized by Dr. Olsson in the chapter): the translation. Obviously, a text should be analyzed only in its original language. A lot of subtleties of the language can be lost in a translation (depending, of course, on the translator), and therefore, the linguist analyzing the text can give a very wrong interpretation of what the original author initially intended to say (or intended to hide).

In regard to the agentive meta-structures, the narrators claim to have seen Mr. U perform two **actions** that, in their view, would incriminate him: "(...) nous avons appris que des Interahamwe, accompagnes d'elements de la Garde Presidentielle sont arrives a la Commune ou ils seront entretenus avec le Bourgmestre (U) et l'Assistant Bourgmestre." (Olsson 2013: 75); "(...) U held an awareness raising meeting... After this meeting the Interahamwe, assisted by the authorities, set about killing...Tutsi[s]" (Olsson 2013: 76).These actions have lead, in the narrators' supposed view, to the **event** (a part of the genocide), Mr. U having a violent **response** after the meeting, supposedly ordering the attack on the Tutsi population. The witnesses/narrators **summarize** and **evaluate** the suspect's alleged actions morally judging them and seeming to highlight the details that, in their mind, show his guilt, using sentences such as "Other local leaders agreed to collaborate with Callixte in the massacres against the Tutsis...namely Charles U" (Olsson 2013: 77) or "He put the ambulance to use in the genocide operation" (Olsson 2013: 78). Whether being manipulated by the people asking the questions, or doing it of their own free will, it seems that the narrators in this case, as in the case before, are trying to trick the reader in thinking that the version they present is the real, *true* one, albeit for different reasons.

As final words, it can be said that the issue of agency can be very difficult to tackle, from a linguistic or any other point of view (especially considering the relatively low number of papers written on this subject). The areas of linguistics that are mostly recommended to be used when dealing with problems of agency/agentivity are semantics (Cruse 1973) (the meaning of words) and pragmatics (the use of language in a social context). With that being said, as Laura M. Ahearn (2001) pointed out, "it is essential that researchers interested in studying language in actual social contexts carefully consider which concept(s) of agency they are employing in their scholarship, lest they allow unsophisticated, possibly contradictory conceptions of action, causality, and responsibility to underpin their work." Needless to say, the forensic linguist should be aware of the problems related to agency, at least on a theoretical level, and exercise a high degree of caution when analyzing any text.

References

1. Ahearn, L. M. (2001) Language and Agency. In *Annual Review of Anthropology,* Vol. 30: 109-137, DOI: 10.1146/annurev.anthro.30.1.109. An adapted and updated version at https://www.academia.edu/1829949/Agency_and_Language.

2. Bamberg, M. (2005) Encyclopaedia entry on 'Agency'. In Herman, D., Jahn, M., & Ryan, M.-L. (eds.). *The Routledge Encyclopedia of Narrative Theory.* New York: Routledge.

3. Cruse, D. A. (1973) Some Thoughts on Agentivity. In *Journal of Linguistics,* Vol. 9, No. 1 (pp. 11-23). Published by: Cambridge University Press. Article Stable URL: http://www.jstor.org/stable/4175175.

4. Emirbayer, M. and Mische, A. (1998) What Is Agency? In *American Journal of Sociology,* Vol. 103, No. 4 (pp. 962-1023). Published by: The University of Chicago Press. Article Stable URL: http://www.jstor.org/stable/10.1086/231294.

5. Olsson, J. (2013) *Wordcrime: Solving Crime Through Forensic Linguistics.* Reprint. London: Bloomsbury Academic.

A SHORT SYNTHESIS OF THE FORENSIC LINGUISTICS PERSPECTIVES ON SEVERAL TYPES OF PLAGIARISM

Ever since the idea of ownership of one's intellectual work began to appear, and the copyright laws have been introduced, plagiarism has been a continuous problem. One of the best ways to detect and prove plagiarism is the use of forensic linguistics. This branch of applied linguistics deals with the application of linguistic methods in the context of the law, studying, among others, the legal language, or, in this case, problems of authorship, trying, for example, to identify whether a text was indeed written by a certain person or not.

First of all, some clarification of the notions is needed. John Olsson makes a clear distinction between plagiarism and copyright infringement. He states that "plagiarism is the unacknowledged use of material authored by someone else, either by taking the precise phrasing of that individual or by rephrasing ideas," being "essentially an academic offense" (Olsson 2013: 23). Copyright infringement, however, "is generally a civil matter ... [it] is a species of plagiarism, but it is the fact that it has specific legal implications that makes us call it 'copyright infringement' rather than 'plagiarism'" (Olsson 2013: 23-24). Sousa-Silva et al. make another distinction, between "intentional and inadvertent plagiarism." They argue that during the learning process, it is possible that students may not be familiar with the rules and regulations regarding citation, or with various texts they are studying (Sousa-Silva et al. 2010). This ignorance would lead to unintentional plagiarism, which should not be punished. Intentional plagiarism (which constitutes an offense), on the other hand, occurs when the plagiarists are fully aware of the rules they are breaking and proceed to do so in order to gain certain benefits.

One example of the type of plagiarism that can be considered copyright infringement is given also by John Olsson. He describes a case he was involved in, namely the Da Vinci Code plagiarism scandal. At the time when the novel was published (in 2004), its author, Dan Brown, was accused by another writer, Lew Perdue, of plagiarizing his books (published in 1983, 1985, and 2000). Olsson gives a detailed description of the work he has done on the case, and although he refrains from giving a final verdict, the evidence he presents is quite clearly leaning toward Perdue being in the right (the actual court verdict was that there was no copyright infringement). One observation made by Olsson is particularly relevant for this case (and for plagiarism, in general). He writes that "when a writer copies the words of another writer, the copy needs to be disguised. This means that the copyist cannot use the same lexicon as the source, but has to adapt words and phrases found in the original. ... The plagiarist has to avoid the very words which come most naturally and which, probably are already in the text being copied. ... [P]lagiarists frequently use words which are much less common than the source author's words to describe something or to talk about something" (Olsson 2013: 31-32).

The following second example of plagiarism, provided by Coulthard et al., is, although different in form, somewhat similar to the previous one. The case discussed in the cited chapter relates to translation plagiarism (someone translating a text and passing it as their own). It is similar to the copyright infringement case in the sense that it uses almost the same tactics to disguise the plagiarism: using other words to express exactly the same idea. Nevertheless, as Coulthard et al. (2013: 531) put it, "it is obviously more difficult to demonstrate plagiarism through translation than same-language plagiarism." According to the cited authors, the key would be to look "first for the evidence of shared content and the very similar sequencing of the content typical of same-language plagiarism." Another interesting type of plagiarism related to translation concerns one translation plagiarizing another translation. Coulthard et al. cite the case of a Spanish translator of Shakespeare's Julius Caesar accusing another translator of plagiarism. The forensic linguist working on that case compared every translation available at that point for that text, looking for shared vocabulary, shared hapax (used only once) words and shared hapax phrases (Coulthard et al. 2013: 531).

A third example of plagiarism involves dictionaries. Here, the plagiarism is more difficult to prove, because, leaving aside the trademarked ones, words by themselves are not under copyright laws, as they do not really "belong" to anyone. Another problem is that many words have only one equivalent in another language, such as the names of plants or animals (Coulthard et al. 2013: 532). An example of such type of plagiarism is given again by Coulthard et al., presenting a Polish case where one publishing house accused another of plagiarizing their dictionary (this being also a case of copyright infringement). The forensic linguist who worked on this case looked at the percentage of shared definitions, of shared spelling mistakes, and of shared wrong definitions, among other criteria. The results were ambiguous. The linguist's conclusions were that either one dictionary plagiarized the other, or they both plagiarized a third, unknown source. At the date of the publication (2013), after nine years of trial, the case was still ongoing.

After presenting several cases of plagiarism, it would be interesting to take a look now at some of the methods used by forensic linguists to detect plagiarism. Two of them are the quantitative and qualitative analysis. These involve statistical work, interpretation of data, stylometric analysis, stylistic analysis, semantic analysis, and many others. There are also various computer applications that can detect plagiarism, up to a certain degree. Many of them can be found online for free, and they are more or less search engines. Their basic function is to search the internet for the specific phrases that were inserted in the search box or uploaded. Other types of applications (that are paid) use a built-in corpus that they search on, besides the internet. All these applications can have their use. However, in regard to electronic plagiarism detection in general, David Woolls points out an important fact: "Computers 'read' text as stream of characters and recognize 'words' by their boundaries: spaces, commas, periods, and the like. Humans ... do much the same.... However, human readers can recognize whole passages from prior reading and knowledge of the subject area, whereas computer programs can only apply rules they are given and can only apply them to the data they have been given". He argues that "it is prudent for the data produced by electronic detection systems to be subject to review by humans" (Woolls 2012: 518).

As final thoughts, this short essay recognizes its limitations. Of course, these are just a few representative examples of types of plagiarism and ways to detect it using forensic linguistics. Plagiarism continues to be a major issue not only in the academic world, but in the publishing world (in general) as well. One solution for that can be forensic linguistics, with its rigorous and effective techniques for the detection and, implicitly, the prevention of plagiarism.

References

1. Coulthard, M. et al. (2013) "Plagiarism: Four forensic linguists' responses to suspected plagiarism." In *The Routledge Handbook of Forensic Linguistics*. Eds. Malcolm Coulthard and Alison Johnson. London: Routledge.

2. Olsson, J. (2013) *Wordcrime: Solving Crime Through Forensic Linguistics*. Reprint. London: Bloomsbury Academic.

3. Sousa-Silva, R. et al. (2010) "'I didn't mean to steal someone else's words!': A Forensic Linguistic Approach to Detecting Intentional Plagiarism." 4th International Plagiarism Conference, 2010. *PlagiarismAdvice.org*.

4. Woolls, D. (2012) "Detecting plagiarism." In *The Oxford Handbook of Language and Law*. Oxford: Oxford University Press.

SHORT CONSIDERATIONS ON THE STANDARDS FOR SCIENTIFIC EXPERT TESTIMONY

With the increasing development of forensic sciences, an urgent need arose to make sure that the evidence presented in court is valid and can shine a new light on the case, bringing a rational objectivity to it through the testimony of expert witnesses. However, until the early 20th century, there was no clear standard for the admission of these expert witnesses.

The Frye guidelines (based on the trial of Frye v. United States, in 1923) were the first important ones that would try to standardize the testimony of expert witnesses. The judge in that case stated that "while the courts will go a long way in admitting experimental testimony deduced from a well-recognized scientific principle or discovery, the thing from which the deduction is made must be sufficiently established to have gained general acceptance in the particular field in which it belongs" (Frye v. United States: 1). Its "general acceptance" rule is however too vague, too general, not flexible enough. It does not explain exactly what is understood by "general acceptance" and does not leave any room for scientific practices that are still experimental and are not widely known, recognized and used. The Frye standard, despite its innovative stance, is deemed to be more or less obsolete nowadays, although it is still used in some American states.

The Daubert guidelines (based on the trial of Daubert v. Merrell Dow Pharmaceuticals, in 1993) improved upon the Frye standard, being more flexible and not as vague. It is easier, when using this standard, to make a decision in regard to admitting scientific expert testimony. The general guidelines in this case are referring to empirical testing (whether the method presented was tested previously and proved to be genuine), peer reviewing and publishing of the method, its known or potential error rate, the standards concerning the performance of the method and the degree to which the theory and technique is generally accepted by a relevant scientific community (Frye v. United States: 2 - 9). The Daubert standard lead to an amendment of the U.S. Rule 702 of the Federal Rules of Evidence in 2000 and later on in 2011, trying to incorporate these guidelines (Federal Rules of Evidence: 30). It is important to emphasize that they are guidelines, and not every point has to be satisfied. The main criticism against it is, however, that it can be used as a checklist by judges that have little or not enough science education, treating the factors as mandatory, thus possibly excluding good forensic experts and possibly including less valuable expert witnesses. The Daubert standard is also not explicit enough so as to not permit attorneys to interpret it in their favor (though that can be said about any law).

The guide issued by the Forensic Science Regulator in 2014 on the legal obligations of expert witnesses in the Criminal Justice System in England and Wales seems to be very detailed, covering about every aspect of expert witness testimony and the Test for Admissibility of Expert Evidence seems to be influenced by the Daubert standard and the Rule 702. It states that "a. The subject-matter is permissible in that a lay person would not be able to form a sound judgement without the expert's assistance; b. The expert's field of expertise is sufficiently well established to pass the ordinary tests of relevance and reliability; c. The expert's opinion, even if not shared by the majority in his field of expertise, has authority because of study and experience of matters outside the jury's knowledge; and d. The witness has sufficient knowledge in the subject to render his opinion of value in resolving the issues before the court" (Legal obligations: 44). The only criticism that I could think of is not exactly against it, but more to how it can be used, just as in the case of the Daubert standard, which is that a judge or a jury without proper scientific training can interpret it very literally.

In conclusion, a standard for scientific expert testimony must be very clear, very explicit, but also flexible enough to allow future scientific discoveries to be admitted as evidence. At the same time, judges and juries should be somewhat educated in scientific matters, in order to be able to make an informed judgement and decision in regard to the admission of expert witnesses for testimony.

References

1. Federal Rules of Evidence (2015), http://federalevidence.com/downloads/rules.of.evidence.pdf. Accessed July 2, 2019.

2. Forensic Science Regulator (2014), Legal obligations, issue 2: January 2014 to January 2015 https://www.gov.uk/government/publications/legal-obligations-issue-2. Accessed July 2, 2019.

3. Frye v. United States, 293 F. 1013 (D C. Cir 1923) http://www.law.ufl.edu/_pdf/faculty/little/topic8.pdf. Accessed July 2, 2019.

FORENSIC LINGUISTICS DISCUSSION ON THE TRANSCRIPTION OF HANDWRITTEN DOCUMENTS

1. Introduction

A transcription helps the forensic linguist see more details and analyze the document more closely. Transcription also helps jurors, attorneys, prosecutors, and judges understand the document better (Solan 1998). A bad transcription could lead to changes in form and meaning, thus leading to an incorrect analysis (Fraser 2003). Transcriptions can be used also for corpora, serving as a database for future cases (Kredens and Coulthard 2012).

In studying handwritten documents such as the Susan Smith confession, the Ramsey note, the James Earl Reed case, or the Gilfoyle case, the author has encountered a few challenges in regard to the forensic transcription of handwritten documents. This is an essential part of a forensic linguist's work, and yet there are no essential studies about it. There seem to be unwritten or implied rules about the forensic transcription of handwritten documents – everyone "knows" how to do it, but there is no actual methodology for it, the focus of most papers or books in this area being on transcriptions of audio or video records, or court proceedings (Fraser 2003; Gibbons 2003; Coulthard and Johnson 2007). Apart from Olsson and Luchjenbroers (2014), who dedicate an entire (albeit short) chapter to forensic transcription, nobody else even mentions the transcription of handwritten documents. Most titles referenced in this paper are only indirectly related to this subject, dealing more with other types of texts, or other types of analysis (Ellen 2005; Hayes 2006; Purdy 2006; Grant 2007; Markle et al. 2011; Harralson 2013). So far there hasn't been any well-organized scientific methodology in regard to this – except in the field of editing of historical documents (Stevens and Burg 1997; Kline and Perdue 2008; Sullivan 2009). Forensic linguistics, as a science, requires such a scientific methodology – at least on a basic level (which transcription is).

This article tries to construct a structured methodology, by studying various other similar methods used in other fields (transcription of historical documents, Handwritten Text Recognition [HTR]) (Lavrenko et al. 2004; Fischer et al. 2009; Romero et al. 2011). As an end goal, the author hopes to bring a more organized approach in regard to the forensic transcription of handwritten documents, satisfying a need for standardization, thus trying to contribute to the resolution of one of the problems that Lawrence Solan (2013: 406) identified, namely that "the forensic community has not adequately developed valid and reliable methods."

2. Literature review

2.1. Forensic linguistics literature

As far as the author has been able to research, the subject of forensic transcription of handwritten documents has not been studied in almost any forensic linguistics book or paper (or in any other forensic literature, for that matter). Coulthard and Johnson (2007: 144-160) mention only the transcription of audio records and handwriting analysis as part of document examination, which McMenamin (2002: 80) defines as being "the scientific study of the physical evidence of a document".

The focus of a forensic document examiner, in the case of handwriting, is on letter size, formation, relative proportions, letter slant, spacing, pressure, connecting strokes, etc. (McMenamin 2002: 81). Gibbons mentions transcriptions, but only in reference to court testimonies (2003: 27-34; 287-288).

As stated previously, the only authors that address this issue are Olsson and Luchjenbroers (2014: 165-169). They enumerate the reasons why a document needs to be transcribed (stylometry, linguistic analysis, adding it to a corpus and making it searchable). Olsson and Luchjenbroers (2014) also list several aims of a transcriptionist. For the purpose of this research, only some parts of the last four are relevant:

"2. To be able to render transcriptions of a variety of written documents to a high standard of accuracy, whether produced in handwriting, on a typewriter, printed, word-processed, or originating as image files.

3. To be able to recognize particular difficulties attached to specific text … including … the transcription of barely legible handwriting…

4. To develop proofreading skills to a high standard to enable (among others) … the proofreading of transcribed handwritten texts, the proofreading of documents for security and disindentification purposes, and the proofreading of scanned documents.

5. To score transcriptions on the basis of confidence in the transcription. It is necessary to do this because in cases where there is illegible or … ambiguous material, the user of the transcription may need to know the degree of

confidence reposed in the transcription by the scribe."
(Olsson and Luchjenbroers 2014: 166)

2.2. Other type of forensic literature

The general forensic literature mentions digital handwriting and forensic handwriting analysis technology (Harralson 2013: 59-69), the variation between normal hand writings (Ellen 2006: 29-31), indented impressions and detection of indented impressions (Ellen 2006: 173-181), identification of handwriting (Purdy, D.C. in Kelly & Lindblom 2006: 47-73; Harralson 2013: 121-124), and forensic handwriting examination (Hayes 2006). The author has found nothing in regard to the actual transcription of handwritten texts.

2.3. Other type of literature dealing with the transcription of handwritten documents

2.3.1. Electronic transcriptions

Nowadays, Optical Character Recognition (OCR) systems are capable of recognizing text with very good accuracy (Ratzlaff 2003; Breuel 2008). The results of the OCR software developed for the automatic transcription of handwritten documents were between 77.12% and 73.91% recognition for the modern IAM database (which contains forms of handwritten English text that can be used to train and test handwritten text recognizers and to perform writer identification and verification experiments, created by the IAM = Institut für Informatik und angewandte Mathematik, Switzerland) (Fischer et al., 2009).

However, according to Romero et al. (2011), OCR products are simply not usable, since in the vast majority of handwritten documents, characters can by no means be isolated automatically (and made searchable). The same authors propose an alternative, the Handwritten Text Recognition (HTR). Their results show that current state of-the-art segmentation-free "off-line HTR" approach produces word error rates of maximum 40% with handwritten old documents (Romero et al. 2011).

Under favorable training conditions some other models achieved a mean word error rate of 0.349, which corresponds to recognition accuracy of 65% (Lavrenko et al. 2004).

As one can see, even though the results of electronic transcription systems are improving, they are still far from perfect. In the author's opinion, the error rate is high enough to be worrisome when dealing with a court case that can jeopardize a person's freedom or even life, thus making these systems unsuitable, currently at least, for forensic linguistics. The error rate might be acceptable for hundreds of pages long documents, where the experts can edit and correct the eventual mistakes in a shorter amount of time than it would take them if the texts would be transcribed by hand, but when dealing with relatively short texts, as in the case of forensic linguistics, it is more convenient to just transcribe them manually – and this, the author believes, leads also to a better understanding of the texts.

2.3.2. The editing of historical documents

Seeing that the author could not find in any forensic literature the needed information to construct the foundation he aimed for, he has started to consider other fields of research that have dealt or are dealing with the transcription of handwritten documents. Reading the published letters of various writers got him thinking about the field of editing, considering that those letters were originally handwritten. In his time of researching this subject, the author has not yet encountered another science or discipline that would study the transcription of handwritten documents, other than documentary editing. He has found that this area of research provides much of the basic methods needed for this type of transcription, and in his opinion they can be applied successfully to the field of forensic linguistics.

First of all, the editing of historical documents provides a very good definition of transcription:

> "Transcription is the process of converting textual and nontextual elements of original documents into readable, publishable, typescript form. In so doing, editors strive to represent original documents faithfully. ... Transcription methods should be presented in an introductory statement and then consistently implemented." (Stevens & Burg 1997: 71)

Stevens and Burg also describe the different types of transcription methods (1997: 72-82):

- Photographic facsimile – this method reproduces the document as an image, or as is, without any kind of interventions.
- Typographical facsimile – reproduces in print the document by mimicking the font and layout of the original.

- Diplomatic transcription – this method transfers the document into modern type, but it indicates through various symbols how the original looked.

- Expanded transcription (and conservative expanded transcription) – comprises a multitude of editing styles, trying to reproduce as faithfully as possible the original manuscript; it is the most "freestyle" of the methods, the transcribers being free to use any style they want, as long as they mention them from the start, and remain consistent throughout the transcription process. The conservative part of this method tries to be even more faithful to the original document by not intervening too much or not at all in the transcription of the text, conveying it as literal as possible, with errors and all.

If Olsson & Luchjenbroers (2014: 166) mention a few of the required aims of a forensic transcriptionist, Kline and Perdue (2008: 116-117) go into much more detail about the work of a transcriptionist in regard to handwritten documents. For this research, the author has considered the following recommendations to be the most important:

- Transcribers should insert a searchable code or symbol in the transcription report for the portions that are illegible to them, making it easier for the editor or analyst to find it later in every transcription.

- Most of the word processors' so-called helpful features (such as AutoCorrect, automatic capitalization, etc.) must be turned off. Also, the text should not be aligned justified, but kept left aligned, and there shouldn't be added any new punctuation, automatic or otherwise.

- When transcribing, proportionally spaced fonts, such as Times New Roman, should be avoided. Instead, the transcriber should use a nonproportional or "fixed" font, such as Courier, in order to see possible spacing problems in the transcription.

Sullivan (2009) adds that the transcriber should make sure that, if the documents to be transcribed are presented as digital images, they are at a very high resolution so that the transcriber would be able to zoom in and see all the details. He also advises that the transcribers should look at similar documents written by the same person, so that they would get a sense of the author's handwriting style, comparing "letters or combinations of letters with those in a known word" and checking "the position, start, middle or end of a word and look for combinations which may be one or more letters" (Sullivan 2009).

3. Uses for forensic linguistics

The recommendations stated by Olsson & Luchjenbroers (2014: 166; 168), detailed in subsection 2.1 of this article, were used as guidelines for the other methods, to see if they can be applied to forensic linguistics.

The most useful, in the author's opinion, would be the expanded transcription method because it meets the requirements for a forensic linguistics transcribed text. The transcription should preserve the peculiarities of the original handwritten text, like nonstandard use of grammar, or punctuation, etc., but it also should be ready for stylometric analysis – meaning the crossed out words should be skipped (at least in the version prepared for stylometric analysis – maybe there should be two or multiple versions of a transcription, to ease even more the understanding of the text). The recommendations given by Sullivan (2009) are also, in the author's opinion, sound and should be taken into consideration. However, as opposed to a historical manuscript editor, the forensic linguist does not need all the details, such as the page presentation, page format, the exact paragraph alignment, etc., the focus being only on the use of language.

The author proposes that a forensic linguistics transcription should be accompanied by a transcription report similar to the one found in the editing historical of historical documents (see the definition of transcription above, as given by Stevens & Burg 1997: 71; also the points made by Kline & Perdue 2008: 116-117, presented above). The report would detail the transcription method(s) used, any particular symbols or signs used, and the reason(s) why all of them were used. This report would help the users of the transcription by letting them know all the details and difficulties that the scribe encountered, in accordance with point #5 made by Olsson & Luchjenbroers (2014: 166, presented above).

4. Case studies

This section will provide some examples of how a transcription report might look, based on the recommendations/methods borrowed from the editing of historical documents. The markings in the transcriptions (detailed in the report) are partially based on Olsson (2005). Naturally, these examples are not to be taken as definitive, everything being subject to improvement.

4.1. The Gilfoyle Case

E. "Paula, Thank you..." 3-4-92

Image 1: Letter from Eddie Gilfoyle to Paula Gilfoyle, 3-4-92. Courtesy of Dr John Olsson

Paula

Thank you for the letter you left me at least
I know the truth now. Ime not bitter and dont
hate you infact I wish you all the luck in the
future.

```
I will be comeing home tonight dont worry I
wont argue or try and talk you out of anything
you have decided.
You can go on Sunday night just make sure(?)
anything you want has gone from the house by
the time I came home on Monday night
I wish you all the luck in the future
We didnt really hit it off anyway
Anything you want to take furniture wise let
me know tonight.
I would like to have our last weekend just the
two of us I will do the garden on Sunday if
weather is ok so you can see what its like
before you go
Good luck
Eddie
```

Transcription report

The expanded transcription method was used in this case because it offers the most editing freedom needed for a forensic linguistics transcription. In short, the idea behind the expanded transcription is that the editor transcribes the handwritten text more or less exactly how the original author would have written it as digital text, with as little changes as possible.

The Courier New font was used because it is monospaced (every character is exactly as wide as every other). This makes it easier for a specialist reader to detect spelling (or any kind of unusual) particularities. The left text alignment was chosen for the same latter reason.

The autocorrect feature was turned off in order to preserve the particularities of the writer's use of the language.

The paragraphs were represented as such in order to increase the readability and to help establish where a sentence ends, since the author did not always use punctuation.

The last word of line 10 in the original text (counting from the date 3-4-92), "sure," marked with a question mark in round parentheses (?) in the transcription, was implied more than understood. This means that the transcriber is unsure if this is the correct word.

There were no other particular symbols or signs used in the original text.

Dear Ed

Yet again, I find it easier talking to you through pen & paper. I know things haven't been good lately and I don't know if it would ever get better. Today is the 1st important day of my life and it's strange I don't know how I feel. I feel happy yet so sad I know you read this to make your mind up, but Ed that feeling of insecurity is always going to be with me. My top + body were like jelly on Tuesday night when you told me there was someone else, even if we were to get back, I will always have that at the back of my mind, going to work, wondering why you were late Ed, or is someone else there is someone else you'd fancy, except to leave me, knowing at the moment you have feelings for someone else. You were the first man who before Tuesday had never looked at another woman, never wanted another woman, how wrong I was, you probably

RF/1/20

...was, she different. At first I thought maybe it was a friendship feeling/relationship but today up confirmed she loved you. How would up feel if I told up I once before loved me. Questions keep flying through + round my head. How did it up this far? How have up told each other your feelings? Have up kissed/touched? Where have up got together to talk? I know I'm torturing myself but I can't help

x

Unfortunately the baby has come when I am at my lowest ever in my life I really don't know what to do; I don't know whether to bring it up myself or put my pride in, move away and give someone else the chance to adopt. I know from today I have got to pick myself up before I lose the little nipper altogether. Whatever I do in 8 months time I will let up know but it was son or daughter.

I still love up more than ever, that hurts. I bet you up said this woman thing has been going on for 5 months. I also

here.

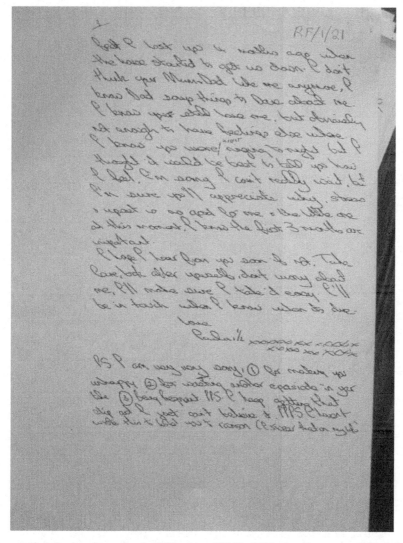

Image 2-4: Letter from Paula Gilfoyle to Eddie Gilfoyle. Courtesy of Dr John Olsson

Dear Ed

Yet again, I find it easier talkin to you
through pen & paper. I know things haven't
been good lately and I don't know if it would

ever get better. Today is the 2nd important day of my life, and it's strange I don't know how I feel. I feel happy yet so sad. I know you need time to make your mind up, but Ed that feeling of insecuirty is always going to be with me. My legs & body wore like jelly on Tuesday night when you told me there was someone else, even if we were to get back, I will always have that at the back of my mind. going to work, wondering why you were late (if you were) wondering if there is anyone else you'd fancy, enough to leave me, knowing at the moment you have feelings for someone else. You wore the first man [(out of all the others(?))] who before Tuesday had never looked at another woman never wanted another woman. how wrong I was, you probably (…) we – so different. At first I thought maybe it was a friendship feeling/relationship but today you confirmed she loved you. how would you feel if I told you some bloke loved me. Questions keep flying through & round my head. How did it go this boy(?)? How have you told each other your feelings? Have you kissed/touched? Where have you got together to talk? I know I'm torturing myself but I can't help it.

Unfortunately the baby has come when I was at my lowest ever in my life. I really didn't know what to do. I don't know whether to bring it up myself or pack my poo in, move away and give someone the chance to adopt. I know from to-day I have got to pick myself up before I lose the little ripper altogether. Whatever I do in 8 months time I will let you know what it was son or daughter.

I still love you more than ever, that hurts so(?) funny you said this woman thing has been going on for 5 months. I also felt I lost you 4 months ago when the house started to get us down. I don't think your Mum & Dad like me anymore, I know Dad says things to Dave about me. I know you still love me, but obviously not enough to have feelings else where. I know you were [right] riging to-night but I thought it would be best to tell you how I feel, I'm sorry I can't really wait, but I'm sure you'll appreciate why, stress & upset is no good for me & the little one at this moment, I know the first 3 months are important.

I hope I hear from you soon if not. Take Care, look after yourself, don't worry about me, I'll make sure I take it easy. I'll be in touch when I know when its due.

```
Love
Paula1½ xxxxxxxxxxxxxxxxxxxxxx
P.S. I am very very sorry, 1) for making you
unhappy 2) for wasting another epasiode in
your life 3)Being Pregnant. PP.S. I keep
getting that slip out I just can't believe it.
P.PP.S I haven't wrote this to hold you to
ranson (I swear that on my life)
```

Transcription report

The expanded transcription method was used because it offers the most editing freedom needed for a forensic linguistics transcription. In short, the idea behind the expanded transcription is that the editor transcribes the handwritten text more or less exactly how the original author would have written it as digital text, with as little changes as possible.

The Courier New font was used because it is monospaced (every character is exactly as wide as every other). This makes it easier for a specialist reader to detect spelling (or any kind of unusual) particularities. The left text alignment was chosen for the same latter reason.

The autocorrect feature was turned off in order to preserve the particularities of the writer's use of the language.

The paragraphs were represented as such in order to increase the readability.

There was one crossed out letter (page 3 of the original text, line 5, the third word) that the transcriber skipped because it is irrelevant for a forensic linguistics analysis.

There were two instances where the original author inserted words above the line, marked in the transcription by [square parentheses]:

- o Page 1, line 20 (counting from the opening line, "Dear Paul"), between the penultimate and the last word, put in (round parentheses) in the original text.

- o Page 3, line 7, between the fourth and the fifth word.

There were four instances where the transcriber was unsure if that is the correct word, or did not understand, or was unable to see the word:

- o The word "others," inserted between the penultimate and the last word of line 20 (counting from the opening line, "Dear Paul"), page 1 in the original text, was implied more than understood, because it is partially outside the margin of the photocopy. It was marked with a question mark in round parentheses (?) in the transcription.

- o It appears to be one or multiple words missing between the end of page 1 and the beginning of page 2 in the original text, because the sentence doesn't seem to make sense. The presumed missing word or words were represented in the transcription by an ellipsis in round parentheses (…).

- o The second word of line 7, on page 2 in the original text was guessed more than understood. It was marked with a question mark in round parentheses (?) in the transcription.

- o The first word of line 23, on page 2 in the original text was impossible to see because it is completely outside the margin of the photocopy, thus it was implied, in order for the sentence to make sense. It was marked with a question mark in round parentheses (?) in the transcription.

Special signs and symbols:

o   The ampersand (&) symbol was used six times in the original text and was reproduced as such in the transcription.

o   At the end of the signature, in the original text, there were added the fraction 1½ one time and the letter "X" twenty-two times, reproduced as such in the transcription.

4.2. The JonBenét Ramsey Case

Mr. Ramsey,

Listen carefully! We are a group of individuals that represent a small foreign faction. We do respect your bussiness but not the country that it serves. At this time we have your daughter in our posession. She is safe and unharmed and if you want her to see 1997, you must follow our instructions to the letter.

You will withdraw $118,000.00 from your account. $100,000 will be in $100 bills and the remaining $18,000 in $20 bills. Make sure that you bring an adequate size attache to the bank. When you get home you will put the money in a brown paper bag. I will call you between 8 and 10 am tomorrow to instruct you on delivery. The delivery will be exhausting so I advise you to be rested. If we monitor you getting the money early, we might call you early to arrange an earlier delivery of the money and hence a earlier delivery pick-up of your daughter.

Any deviation of my instructions will result in the immediate execution of your daughter. You will also be denied her remains for proper burial. The two gentlemen watching over your daughter do not particularly like you so I advise you not to provoke them. Speaking to anyone about your situation, such as Police, F.B.I., etc., will result in your daughter being beheaded. If we catch you talking to a stray dog, she dies. If you alert bank authorities, she dies. If the money is in any way marked or tampered with, she dies. You will be scanned for electronic devices and if any are found, she dies. You can try to deceive us but be warned that we are familiar with law enforcement countermeasures and tactics. You stand a 99% chance of killing your daughter if you try to out smart us. Follow our instructions and you stand a 100% chance of getting her back. You and your family are under constant scrutiny as well as the authorities. Don't try to grow a brain John. You are not the only fat cat around so don't think that killing will be difficult. Don't underestimate us John. Use that good southern common sense of yours. It is up to you now John!

Victory!
S.B.T.C

Image 5: Letter to JonBenét Ramsey's father. Courtesy of Dr John Olsson

Mr. Ramsey,

Listen carefully! We are a group of individuals that represent a small foreign faction. We respect your bussiness but not the country that it serves. At this time we have your daughter in our posession. She is safe and unharmed and if you want her to see 1997, you must follow our instructions to the letter.

You will withdraw $118,000.00 from your account. $100,000 will be in $100 bills and the remaining $18,000 in $20 bills. Make sure that you bring an adequate size attache to the bank. When you get home you will put the money in a brown paper bag. I will call you between 8 and 10 am tomorrow to instruct you on delivery. The delivery will be exhausting so I advise you to be rested. If we monitor you getting the money early, we might call you early to arrange an earlier delivery of the money and hence a earlier pick-up of your daughter.

Any deviation of my instructions will result in the immediate execution of your daughter. You will also be denied her remains for proper burial. The two gentlemen watching over your daughter do not particularly like you so I advise you not to provoke them. Speaking to anyone about your situation, such as Police, F.B.I., etc., will result in your daughter being beheaded. If we catch you talking to a stray dog, she dies. If you alert bank authorities, she dies. If the money is in any way marked or tampered with, she dies. You will be scanned for electronic devices and if any are found, she dies. You can try to deceive us, but be warned that we are familiar with Law enforcement countermeasures and tactics. You stand a 99% chance of killing your daughter if you try to out smart us. Follow our instructions and you stand 100% chance of getting her back. You and your family are under constant scrutiny as well as the authorities. Don't try to grow a brain John. You are not the only fat cat around so don't think that killing will be difficult. Don't underestimate us John. Use that good southern common sense of yours. It is up to you now John!

Victory!

S.B.T.C.

Transcription report

The expanded transcription method was used because it offers the most editing freedom needed for a forensic linguistics transcription. In short, the idea behind the expanded transcription is that the editor transcribes the handwritten text more or less exactly how the original author would have written it as digital text, with as little changes as possible.

The Courier New font was used because it is monospaced (every character is exactly as wide as every other). This makes it easier for a specialist reader to detect spelling (or any kind of unusual) particularities. The left text alignment was chosen for the same latter reason.

The autocorrect feature was turned off in order to preserve the particularities of the writer's use of the language.

The paragraphs were represented as such in order to increase the readability of the transcription.

There were two crossed out words (page 1 of the original text, the last word of line 4, counted from the starting line "Mr Ramsey," and page 2, the first word of the second line) that the transcriber skipped because they were irrelevant for a forensic linguistics analysis.

There were no other particular symbols or signs used in the original text.

4.3. The James Earl Reed Case

Image 6: Letter from James Earl Reed, page 4. Courtesy of Dr John Olsson

PHILLIP ALL THESE LAWYERS CARE ABOUT ARE
IF YOU ARE GUILTY TO KEEP YOU A LIVE AS LONG
AS POSSIBLE OR GET YOU A LIFE SENTENCE ALSO IF
YOU ARE INNOCENCE IS TO HIDE YOUR INNOCENCE

ALONG WITH KEEPING YOU UPON DEATH ROW AS LONG
AS POSSIBLE ALONG WITH TO PUT YOU IN A TRAP
THAT WILL COVER-UP YOUR INNOCENCE ALONG WITH
TRAP YOU INTO THE APPEAL SYSTEM EXACTLY AS
THEY WOULD HAVE HAD ME NOW IF I WOULDNT HAVE
DONE EXACTLY WHAT EXACTLY WHAT GOD HAD ME TO
TAKE THE STAND & FOR IF I WOULD HAVE ALREADY
BEEN TURN DOWN BY THE SC SUPREME COURT WHICH
THERE GOES MY INNOCENCE AND INTO THE APPEAL
TRAP REMAINING UPON DEATH ROW 15-20 YEARS
LOOKING GUILTY SOUNDING GUILTY GOING TO
EXECUTION THIS IS EXACTLY HOW THEY DO THE
LAWYERS DO THESE GUY YET I AM THE ONLY
INNOCENCE ONE WHO HAVE BEEN FIGHTING MY
INNOCENCE WHO HAVE PROVEN MY INNOCENCE NOW WHO
HAVE TAKEN A STAND UPON MY INNOCENCE THE OTHER
GUYS ARENT DOING ANYTHING TO HELP THEMSELF
NOTHING!

PHILLIP YOU KNOW THAT I AM ABLE TO SHOW
ABLE TO PROVE EVERYTHING I WRITE OR SAY WHICH
THESE LAWYERS KNOW THIS AS WELL FOR THAT IS
WHY THEY DO THE BEST TO DISCOURAGE ME FROM
FIGHTING

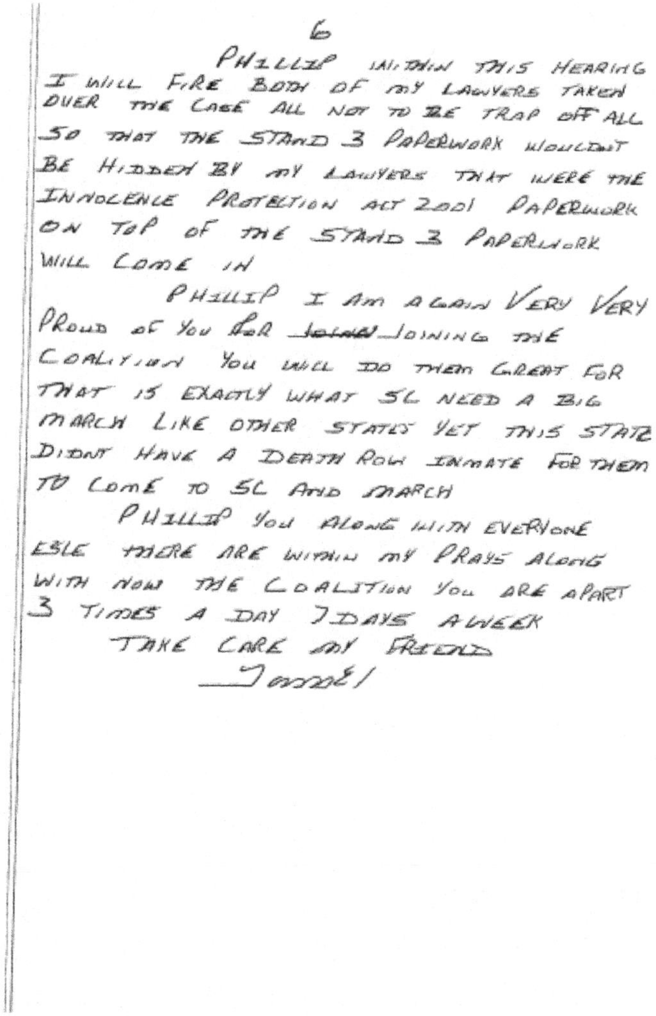

Image 7: Letter from James Earl Reed, page 6. Courtesy of Dr John Olsson

PHILLIP WITHIN THIS HEARING I WILL FIRE
BOTH OF MY LAWYERS TAKEN OVER THE CASE ALL NOT
TO BE TRAP OF ALL SO THAT THE STAND &
PAPERWORK WOULDNT BE HIDDEN BY MY LAWYERS THAT

```
WERE THE INNOCENCE PROTECTION ACT 2001
PAPERWORK ON TOP OF THE STAND & PAPERWORK WILL
COME IN
     PHILLIP I AM AGAIN VERY VERY PROUD OF YOU
FOR JOINING THE COALITION YOU WILL DO THEM
GREAT FOR THAT IS EXACTLY WHAT SC NEED A BIG
MARCH LIKE OTHER STATES YET THIS STATE DIDNT
HAVE A DEATH ROW INMATE FOR THEM TO COME TO SC
AND MARCH
     PHILLIP YOU ALONG WITH EVERYONE ESLE THERE
ARE WITHIN MY PRAYS ALONG WITH NOW THE
COALITION YOU ARE APART 3 TIMES A DAY 7 DAYS A
WEEK
     TAKE CARE MY FRIEND
     JamesE /
```

Transcription report

The expanded transcription method was used because it offers the most editing freedom needed for a forensic linguistics transcription. In short, the idea behind the expanded transcription is that the editor transcribes the handwritten text more or less exactly how the original author would have written it as digital text, with as little changes as possible.

The Courier New font was used because it is monospaced (every character is exactly as wide as every other). This makes it easier for a specialist reader to detect spelling (or any kind of unusual) particularities. The left text alignment was chosen for the same latter reason.

The autocorrect feature was turned off in order to preserve the particularities of the writer's use of the language.

The paragraphs were represented as such in order to increase the readability and to help establish where a sentence ends, since the original author did not use punctuation, except for one exclamation mark (page 4, line 26).

There was one crossed out word (page 6 of the original text, line 10, the fifth word) that the transcriber skipped because it was irrelevant for a forensic linguistics analysis.

There were no other particular symbols or signs used in the original text.

4.4. The Susan Smith Case

When I left my home on Tuesday, October 25, I was very emotionally distraught. I didn't want to live anymore! I felt like things could never get any worse. When I left home, I was going to ride around a little while and then go to my mom's. As I rode and rode and rode, I felt even more anxiety coming upon me about not wanting to live. I felt I couldn't be a good mom anymore but I didn't want my children to grow up without a mom. I felt I had to end our lives to protect us all from any grief or harm. ▓▓▓▓▓▓▓▓▓▓▓ I had never felt so lonely and so sad in my entire life. I was in love with someone. very much, but he didn't love me and never would. I had a very difficult time accepting that. But I had hurt him very much and I could see why he could never love me. When I was @ John D. Long Lake, ▓▓▓▓▓ I had never felt so scared and unsure as I did then. I wanted to end my life so bad and was in my car ready to go down that ramp into the water and I did go part way, but I stopped. I went again and stopped. I then got out of the car and ▓▓ stood by the car a nervous wreck. Why was I feeling this way? Why was everything so bad in my life? I had no answers to these questions. I dropped to the lowest when I allowed my children to go down that ramp into the water without me. I took off running and screaming "Oh God! Oh God, NO!" What have I done? Why did you let this happen? I wanted to turn around so bad and go back, but I knew it was too late. I was an absolute mental case! I couldn't believe what I had done. I love my children w/ all my ♥. That will never change. I have prayed to them for forgiveness and hope that they will find it in their ♥ to forgive me. I never

meant to hurt them!! I am ~~sorry~~ for what
has happened and I know that I need some
help. I don't think I will ever be able to
forgive myself for what I have done. My children,
Michael and Alex, are with our Heavenly Father
now and I know that they will never be hurt
again. As a mom, that means more than words
could ever say.

I knew from day one. the truth would prevail,
but I was so scared I didn't know what to
do. It was very tough emotionally to sit and watch
my family hurt like they did. It was time to bring
a 'peace' of mind to everyone, including myself. My
children deserve to have the best and now they
will. I broke down on Thursday, November 3 and
told Sheriff Howard Wells the truth. It wasn't
easy, but after the truth was out, I felt like
the world was lifted off my shoulders. I know
now that it is going to be a tough and long
road ahead of me. At this very moment, I don't
feel I will be able to handle what's coming, but
I have prayed to God that he give me the
strength to survive each day and to face these
times and situations in my life that will be
extremely painful. I have put my total faith in
God and He will take care of me.

Susan V. Smith
11/3/94
5:05 p.m.

WITNESS

Cur D. Alfian, 7151, Caciniville, S.C.
Tommy Pagan, SLED, Calyse

Image 8-9: The Susan Smith confession. Courtesy of Dr John Olsson

When I left my home on Tuesday, October 25, I
was very emotionally distraught. I didn't want
to live anymore! I felt like things could
never get any worse. When I left home, I was
going to ride around a little while and when

go to my mom's. As I rode and rode and rode, I felt even more anxiety coming upon me about not wanting to live. I felt I couldn't be a good mom anymore but I didn't want my children to grow up without a mom. I felt I had to end our lives to protect us all from any grief or harm. I had never felt so lonely and so sad in my entire life. I was in love with someone very much, but he didn't love me and never would. I had a very difficult time accepting that. But I had hurt him very much and I could see why he could never love me. When I was @ John D. Long Lake, I had never felt so scared and unsure as I did then. I wanted to end my life so bad and was in my car ready to go down that ramp into the water and I did go part way, but I stopped. I went again and stopped. I then got out of the car and stood by the car [a] nervous wreck. Why was I feeling this way? Why was everything so bad in my life? I had no answers to these questions. I dropped to the lowest when I allowed my children to go down that ramp into the water without me. I took off running and screaming "Oh God! Oh God, NO!" What have I done? Why did you let this happen? I wanted to turn around so bad and go back, but I knew it was too late. I was an absolute mental case! I couldn't believe what I had done. I love my children w/ all my ♥. That will never change. I have prayed to them for forgiveness and hope that they will find it in there ♥ to forgive me. I never meant to hurt them!! I am **sorry** for what has happened and I know that I need some help. I don't think I will ever be able to forgive myself for what I have done. My children, Michael and Alex, are with our Heavenly Father now and I know that they will never be hurt again. As a mom, that means more than words could ever say.

I knew from day one, the truth will prevail, but I was so scared I didn't know what to do. It was very tough emotionally to sit and watch my family hurt like they did. It was time to bring a piece of mind to everyone, including myself. My children deserve to have the best and now they will. I broke down on Thursday, November 3 and told Sheriff Howard Wells the truth. It wasn't easy, but after the truth was out, I felt like the world was lifted off my shoulders. I know now that it is going to be a tough and long road ahead of me. At this very moment, I don't feel I will be able to handle

```
what's coming, but I have prayed to God that
he give me the strength to survive each day
and to face those times and situations in my
life that will be extremely painful. I have
put my total faith in God and He will take
care of me.
Susan V. Smith
```

Transcription report

The expanded transcription method was used because it offers the most editing freedom needed for a forensic linguistics transcription. In short, the idea behind the expanded transcription is that the editor transcribes the handwritten text more or less exactly how the original author would have written it as digital text, with as little changes as possible.

The Courier New font was used because it is monospaced (every character is exactly as wide as every other). This makes it easier for a specialist reader to detect spelling (or any kind of unusual) particularities. The left text alignment was chosen for the same latter reason.

The autocorrect feature was turned off in order to preserve the particularities of the writer's use of the language.

The paragraphs were represented as such in order to increase the readability.

There were several crossed-out words in the original text: on page 1, line 11, the third word(s); on page 1, line 17, the fifth word; on page 1, line 22, the ninth word that the transcriber skipped because they were irrelevant for a forensic linguistics analysis.

The original author underlined two words: on page 1, line 12, the last word (transcribed as <u>underlined</u>); and on page 2, line 1, the seventh word, which was underlined multiple times, and was transcribed in **<u>bold and underlined</u>**.

There was one instance where the original author inserted one word above the line, marked in the transcription by [square parentheses]: page 1, line 23, between the first and the second words.

The author used two special symbols in the original text: the "at" symbol "@" (used one time, on page 1, line 16, the last character) and the heart symbol "♥" (used two times on page 1: line 33, the seventh character, and line 35, the eighth character), transcribed as such.

5. Conclusions

1. The well documented and tested methods used by the editing of historical documents can be of use for a forensic linguist in transcribing handwritten documents, and should be adopted, as there is no current actual scientific methodology for this.

2. An official transcription report from a professional transcriber would help establish a reliable professional relationship between the scribe and the beneficiary of the transcription. It would also help create a reliable scientific methodology that can be used in court.

3. It is preferable to use manual transcription instead of OCR or other software of this type because generally, most texts that a forensic linguist has to work with are relatively short. The software would be useful in cases where there are large

amounts of text – but even then, it could be problematic because of its inability to recognize all handwritten characters (some people having worse handwriting than others), and because of its current relatively high error rate.

6. References

1. Coulthard, M. and Johnson, A. (2007) *An introduction to forensic linguistics: language in evidence*. London: Routledge.

2. Ellen, D. (2006) *Scientific Examination of Documents: Methods and Techniques, Third Edition (International Forensic Science and Investigation)*. CRC Press

3. Fischer, A., Wuthrich, M., Liwicki, M., Frinken, V., Bunke, H., Viehhauser, G., and Stolz, M. (2009) Automatic Transcription of Handwritten Medieval Documents. In *Virtual Systems and Multimedia. VSMM '09. 15th International Conference on*, pp.137-142.

4. Fraser, H. (2003) Issues in transcription: factors affecting the reliability of transcripts as evidence in legal cases. In *Forensic Linguistics* 10(2).

5. Gibbons, J. (2003) *Forensic linguistics: an introduction to language in the justice system*. Oxford: Blackwell.

6. Grant, T. (2007) Quantifying evidence in forensic authorship analysis. In *The International Journal of Speech, Language and the Law* 14(1): 1-25. https://doi:10.1558/ijsll.v14i1.1

7. Harralson, H.H. (2013) *Developments in Handwriting and Signature Identification in the Digital Age (Forensic Studies for Criminal Justice)*. London: Routledge.

8. Hayes, R. C. (2006) *Forensic Handwriting Examination: A Definitive Guide*. ReedWrite Press.

9. Kline, M.-J. and Perdue, S.H. (2008) *A Guide to Documentary Editing*. Charlottesville, VA: University of Virginia Press.

10. Kredens, K. and Coulthard, M. (2012) Corpus linguistics in authorship identification. In *The Oxford Handbook of Language and Law*. Oxford: Oxford University Press.

11. Lavrenko, V., Rath, T.M., and Manmatha, R. (2004) Holistic word recognition for handwritten historical documents. In *Document Image Analysis for Libraries. Proceedings. First International Workshop on*, pp. 278-287

12. Markle, D.T., West, R.E., and Rich, P.J. (2011) Beyond Transcription: Technology, Change, and Refinement of Method. In *Forum: Qualitative Social Research* 12(3).

13. McMenamin, G.R. (2002) *Forensic Linguistics: Advances in Forensic Stylistics*. CRC Press.

14. Olsson, J. (2005) *Forensic Transcription Course*. Unpublished.

15. Olsson, J. and Luchjenbroers, J. (2014) *Forensic linguistics. Third edition*. London: Bloomsbury Academic.

16. Purdy, D.C. (2006) Identification of Handwriting. In Kelly, J.S. and Lindblom, B.S. (eds.) *Scientific Examination of Questioned Documents, Second Edition (Forensic and Police Science Series)*. CRC Press.

17. Romero, V., Serrano, N., Toselli, A.H., Sánchez, J.A., and Vidal, E. (2011) Handwritten Text Recognition for Historical Documents. In *Proceedings of Language Technologies for Digital*

Humanities and Cultural Heritage Workshop, pp. 90–96, Hissar, Bulgaria, 16 September 2011.

18. Solan, L.M. (1998) Linguistic experts as semantic tour guides. In *Forensic Linguistics* 5(2).

19. Solan, L.M. (2013) The forensic linguist: The expert linguist meets the adversarial system. In Coulthard, M. and Johnson, A. (eds.) *The Routledge Handbook of Forensic Linguistics*. London: Routledge.

20. Stevens, M.E. and Burg, S.B. (1997) *Editing Historical Documents: A Handbook of Practice*. AltaMira Press / AASLH

21. Sullivan, F. (2009) *Useful Tips for Reading Handwritten Documents*. [Online] Available from: http://archivesoutside.records.nsw.gov.au/useful-tips-for-reading-handwritten-documents/ [Accessed: July 16, 2019].

Legal references:

U.K.

R v Norman Edward Gilfoyle, 1993; Case No: 990180053

U.S.A.

The State of South Carolina v James Earl Reed, 1996; 332 S.C. 35, 503 S.E.2d 747

The State of South Carolina v Susan Vaughan Smith, 1995; 94-GS-44-906 and 94-GS-44-907

IDENTIFYING AN AUTHOR'S NATIVE LANGUAGE THROUGH THE USE OF PUNCTUATION

1. Introduction

The study of punctuation is generally not considered to be that important outside of academia. When teaching another language, educators put more emphasis on grammar and spelling, and less on punctuation (many foreign language manuals do not even mention it). Thus, a person can achieve perfect command of a foreign language's grammar and spelling, but still keep some uses of their native language punctuation in their writing. The present research deals with some aspects of language that a person learns to use and applies since early childhood every day without even thinking, and which might escape them when using another language. If there is a definition that this study is based on, it is the Second Language Acquisition (SLA) definition of *error* (Corder 1967; Ellis 1994: 47-72, 700-701; Gass & Selinker 2008: 102-110), which will be detailed in the **Literature review** section.

In forensic linguistics, punctuation was found to be a marker that can be used in authorship analyses in conjunction with other markers (Chaski 2001, 2005, 2007, 2012; Coulthard and Johnson 2007; Coulthard 2013; Eagleson 1990; Ishihara 2017; McMenamin 2002; Michell 2013; Narayanan et al. 2012; Olsson 2013; Pestian et al. 2010; Prokofyeva 2013; Woolls 2013), trying to prove plagiarism (Coulthard et al. 2013; Sousa-Silva 2014), among others. However, each language has its punctuation rules (Lupescu 2016; Mortara Garavelli 2003; Popa and

Popa 2015; Quirk et al. 2005; Ramat and Muller 2009; Riegel et al. 2015; Serianni et al. 2017; Stan 2015; Trask 1997). Therefore, theoretically at least, it could be possible for one to identify an author's native language through punctuation, in conjunction with other analyses, of course.

The paper will analyze how and if French, Italian, and Romanian uses of punctuation can be identified in American English. This will be an expansion of a previous research of the author concerning the punctuation differences between American English, French, and Romanian (Lupescu 2016). The author has found that the main distinctions are in regard to the quotation marks, the comma, and the dash. In many cases, one language would use certain punctuation signs where another language would use others. Another important dissimilitude is that French uses spaces around several punctuation signs – the quotation marks, the exclamation and question marks, the slash, the semicolon, and the colon (Ramat and Muller 2009: 89).

The punctuation rules presented here are based on descriptive grammars that describe the most common uses of the language. This research deals only with American English, as there are also some differences in the use of punctuation between British English and American English (Quirk et al. 2005: 19). The French punctuation norms presented in this study are the ones used mostly in France.

Due to the nature of the translator-client copyright and other type of clauses, the author was unable to use any of the translations he has done or is in possession of. The author has used some of the examples he has provided in the previous research because they were either already published, attributed translations or translations done by him solely for that research (thus belonging to him), in order to explain how the punctuation should be used, as close as possible to a native-level use of language.

To study how punctuation is employed in a context that is closer to everyday use, the author has utilized the ParaCrawl Corpus version 1.0 (Koehn et al. 2018), a free collection of large parallel corpora to/from English for all the official languages of the European Union (which co-financed the project). The creators use their own open-source software to search and index bilingual content on the internet. The language pair corpora can be downloaded individually (in this case, French / English, Italian / English, and Romanian / English) as an archive that contains two searchable files: one for English, one for the other language. This was very important, because the study required a search for the influence of other languages in English texts only (many other bilingual or multilingual corpora contain only one searchable file that combine both languages). Unfortunately, ParaCrawl does not distinguish between American and British (or any other type of) English, or between Canadian and France (or any other kind of) French – the choice is just generic "English" or "French"; it is up to the user to make the distinction.

2. Literature review

One of the earliest examples of an expert linguist using punctuation in conjunction with other methods to identify an author was R.D. Eagleson, in 1990. Currently, there are two approaches in forensic linguistics that Lawrence Solan (2013) names "algorithmic" (that make extensive or exclusive use of specialized software to investigate the texts; sometimes called Natural Language Processing/NLP studies or computational forensic linguistics [Wools 2013: 576]) and "intuitive" (that use more "traditional" methods to study the texts, such as forensic stylistics and others, relying more on human, rather than machine expertise). The best known linguists to use punctuation prominently in their authorship analyses are Carole Chaski (2001, 2005, 2007, 2012), an exponent of the "algorithmic" approach with her proprietary software ALIAS (Automated Linguistic Identification and Assessment System), and Gerald McMenamin (2002, 2013), a proponent of the "intuitive" approach. Both parties have criticized each other's methods and reliability of the results (Chaski 2001, 2012: 499-500; Grant & Baker 2001; McMenamin 2001, 2002: 173, 2013: 505-506), but every expert agrees on using punctuation in their author identification studies, in conjunction with other markers. As Wools (2013: 577) stated, "… it is usually not desirable to simply ignore the punctuation, because the use of punctuation is a structural decision made by a writer and as such can be distinctive."

Carole Chaski sees punctuation as "a graphic (nonverbal) reflection of syntactic structure" (2001). Her approach to punctuation (using ALIAS) is syntactically-classified, meaning the punctuation signs are analyzed based on the syntactic edge they are marking (Chaski 2005). Though highly important for forensic linguistics in general, her research does not really help this study, as it doesn't distinguish between the (syntactic or otherwise) use of punctuation of authors that have a different native language other than English.

Gerald McMenamin identifies punctuation as a style marker, giving an extensive list from his experience (2002: 220-223). There are also four chapters in his 2002 book that might have been of interest for this research: four stylistic studies for different languages (Spanish, Gujarati, Korean, and Japanese) that were written by experts in those languages, each of them identifying punctuation as a style marker. The Spanish language section was written by McMenamin (2002: 233-267), citing also linguist Alcala Arevalo (1991: 202) in regard to punctuation (2002: 236); P.J. Mistry wrote the Gujarati language section (2002: 269-278); Dongdoo Choi, the Korean section (2002: 279-294); and Wakado Yasuda, the Japanese one (2002: 295-311). However, none of them present any differences between any languages in regard to the use of punctuation (which is mentioned only as being a style identifier that is used in authorship studies). An exception might take Yasuda (2002: 300), but only with a few sentences, in which he explains certain particularities of the Japanese use of punctuation.

In more recent years, forensic linguists have been using punctuation in algorithmic and "intuitive" studies to identify genuine suicide notes (e.g. Pestian et al. 2010, Prokofyeva 2013), or for authorship attribution (Narayanan et al. 2012, Michell 2013, Olsson 2013, Ishihara 2017, among many others). Rico-Sulayes (2011) uses punctuation applying Chaski's methods in an algorithmic study on

Spanish language. Unfortunately, he does not mention any differences between languages, or any peculiarities of the Spanish use of punctuation. An interesting paper that deals with interlingual problems is Sousa-Silva's (2014), regarding translingual plagiarism, though he doesn't use punctuation per se in his study, only mentioning it in passing.

Several interlingual theories are discussed in many other forensic linguistics studies. Eades (2013: 411-422) and Patrick (2012: 533-546) talk about Language Analysis in the Determination of Origin (LADO) (also called *linguistic identification*), which is a field of study concerned with determining the country of origin of an asylum seeker. However, this kind of research is based mostly on vocal production and the study of accents, with very little emphasis on the analysis of texts, not to mention punctuation. Tetreault et al. (2012) discuss the NLP field of Native Language Identification (NLI), the task of automatic identification of a speaker's first language based solely on the speaker's writing in another language. Unfortunately, this paper also does not contain anything about punctuation. Perkins and Grant (2018), on the other hand, do use punctuation in their study, examining "the potential use of interlingual identifiers for forensic authorship analysis and native language influence detection (NLID)." The focus of NLID, as they define it, is to identify influence from one language (L1) on an anonymous author's writing in another language (L2). They prefer the terminology *"influence detection* over that of *identification* as it acknowledges the probability that any L2 might be influenced by several languages rather than a single L1" (Perkins and Grant 2018). The authors, nonetheless, do not give any details about punctuation that could serve the present study (such as how much it weighs in the final result, how much it can be used as a marker, or how much it gives away an author's native language).

One interlingual research field that has helped this research is Second Language Acquisition (SLA), particularly its studies of *errors*. S.P. Corder (1967) was the first linguist to make the difference between *mistakes* and *errors*. According to him, a *mistake* is when the user (or the learner of the language) is aware of their deviation from the norm and is able to correct it immediately, or soon thereafter. In contrast, an *error* is when the learner is not aware of the deviation, using the language in a way they are accustomed to, according to the rules of their own language (Corder 1967). Ellis (1994: 701) differentiates further: "An error can be overt (the deviation is apparent in the surface form of the utterance) or covert (the deviation is only evident when the learner's meaning intention is taken into account)." Gass & Selinker (2008: 102-103) point out that "An error ... is systematic. That is, it is likely to occur repeatedly and is not recognized by the learner as an error. The learner in this case has incorporated a particular erroneous form (from the perspective of the [target language]) into his or her system. Viewed in this way, errors are only errors from a teacher's or researcher's perspective, not from the learner's." This attribute of the error has helped this research in identifying the influences of other languages in American English: if the non-standard form is used multiple times, it's an error, not a mistake. Also, in the case of the present study, punctuation errors made by natives of other languages when using American English can be considered covert, as they might not be as obvious as other type of errors, and can reflect a system that they have learned and used previously in their own language (for details see the next section, **3. Punctuation as used in American English, French, Italian, and Romanian**). In that regard, Ellis (1994: 48) cites Lee (1957), who speaks of an analysis of 2000 errors in the writing of Czechoslovakian learners, including wrong punctuation.

To return to forensic linguistics, Coulthard and Johnson also mention the distinction between mistakes and errors, pointing out that "Both ... can be useful authorship markers" (2007: 171), with Coulthard (2013) writing about one of his analyses where he used mistakes and errors as markers of authorship.

3. Punctuation as used in American English, French, Italian, and Romanian

Note: All the French, Italian, and Romanian translations presented in the *Examples* sections are the author's, except for *The Little Prince* [*Examples (2)*].

3.1. The Quotation Marks

It is considered standard in American English for other punctuation signs, such as periods and commas, to be placed within quotations (Quirk et al. 2005: 19, 1630; Trask 1997: 103-104). A general exception to this rule is the colon. The primary quotation marks in American English are the double inverted commas (" "). In French, their specific quotation marks (« »), the guillemets, are written with a space after the first and before the second. Usually, the primary quotation marks in Italian are the same as the French ones (« »), but without the spaces (Mortara Garavelli 2003: 28-29; Serianni et al. 2017:

55). For **quotation within quotation** (or secondary level), American English generally uses single inverted commas (' ') (Quirk et al. 2005: 1630; Trask 1997: 99-100). French uses double inverted commas (" ") (Ramat and Muller 2009: 94; Riegel et al. 2015: 156-157), and so does Italian (Mortara Garavelli 2003: 30-31). Romanian uses at primary level the curved quotation marks („") and at secondary level, the guillemets (« »), but without the spaces (Stan 2015: 53; Popa and Popa 2015: 450).

Examples (1):

- *American English:* "Low hemoglobin and hematocrit values in active women may not represent true anemia but may instead represent 'sports anemia,' also referred to as 'dilutional pseudoanemia.'" (Harris 2005: 57)

- *French:* « Il est possible qu'une baisse de l'hémoglobine et de l'hématocrite dans les femmes actives n'indique pas une anémie réelle, mais une "anémie du sportif", appelée aussi la "pseudo-anémie dilutionnelle". »

- *Italian:* «I bassi valori di emoglobina ed ematocrito nelle donne attive possono non rappresentare la vera anemia, ma possono invece rappresentare l'"anemia sportiva", detta anche "pseudoanemia diluitiva".»

- *Romanian:* „Este posibil ca valorile scăzute în ceea ce priveşte hemoglobina şi hematocritul din femeile active să nu indice anemie propriu-zisă, ci «anemia sportivului», cunoscută şi sub denumirea de «pseudo-anemie diluţionară»."

The quotation marks in American English are also used to indicate dialogue, encompassing each spoken sentence (direct speech) (Quirk et al. 2005: 1022, 1630; Trask 1997: 95). In French, usually the first line of dialogue starts with guillemets, then each subsequent line of dialogue starts with a dash (Ramat and Muller 2009: 95; Riegel et al. 2015: 161). The end of the dialogue is indicated by closing quotation marks. If only one person speaks, then only quotation marks are used. In Romanian, there are no quotation marks for the dialogue (which is indicated also by dashes) (Stan 2015: 58), but only to indicate that the characters are thinking or speaking to themselves (direct speech) (Popa and Popa 2015: 450). Generally, Italian has almost the same rules as Romanian, the main difference being that the dash also closes the dialogue, before the period or after any other punctuation mark, if the sentence doesn't end (Mortara Garavelli 2003: 32-34); if the line of dialogue isn't followed by any other sentence, the dash doesn't close it. Depending on various editorial choices, Italian does adopt sometimes also the French or the American quotation rules, with the exception that there is no space after and before the guillemets, or the punctuation signs are outside the quotation marks (Mortara Garavelli 2003: 32-34).

Examples (2):

American English:

"I've nothing more to do here," he said to the king. "I'll be off!"

"Don't leave," replied the king, who was so proud to have a subject. "Don't leave, I'm making you a minister!"

"Minister of what?"

"Of... of Justice!" (Saint-Exupéry 2015a: 36)

French:

« Je n'ai plus rien à faire ici, dit-il au roi. Je vais repartir !

— Ne pars pas, répondit le roi qui était si fier d'avoir un sujet. Ne pars pas, je te fais ministre !

— Ministre de quoi ?

— De… de la Justice ! » (Saint-Exupéry 2016a: 44)

Italian:

— Non ho più nulla da fare qui — disse al Re. — Voglio ripartire!

— Non partire, — replicò il Re, che era tanto fiero d'avere un suddito.

— Non partire, ti nomino ministro.

— Ministro di che?

— Della… della giustizia! (Saint-Exupéry 2016b: 31)

Romanian:

— Nu mai am nicio treabă pe-aici – îi spuse regelui. Am să plec mai departe!

— Nu pleca, zise regele, care era nespus de mândru că are un supus. Nu pleca, te fac ministru!

— Ce fel de ministru?

— Al… al justiţiei! (Saint-Exupéry 2015b: 40)

Or, speaking to themselves/thinking (direct speech):

American English:

"Grown-ups are really strange," the little prince thought to himself on his travels. (Saint-Exupéry 2015a: 37)

French:

« Les grandes personnes sont bien étranges », se dit le petit prince, en lui-même, durant son voyage. (Saint-Exupéry 2016a: 45)

Italian:

«Gli adulti sono ben strani» rifletté tra sé e sé il piccolo principe durante il viaggio. (Saint-Exupéry 2016b: 32)

Romanian:

„Oamenii mari sunt atât de ciudați!", îşi spuse micul prinț, continuându-şi călătoria. (Saint-Exupéry 2015b: 41)

3.2. The Comma

The comma is probably the most versatile punctuation mark in all languages, but only a couple differences in its use stand out between French, Italian, Romanian, and American English. One is that American English would use a comma in cases when French and Romanian would use a colon – e.g., when an enumeration follows, or an example, or in direct speech.

Examples (3):

- *American English:*
  - o *Example/enumeration:* Bob likes sports. For example, soccer, hurdling, and long-distance running.
  - o *Direct speech:* He said, "What are you doing?"

- *French:*
    - ○ *Example/enumeration:* Bob aime les sports. Par exemple : le football, la course de haies et la course de fond.
    - ○ *Direct speech:* Il dit : « Qu'est-ce que tu fais ? »
- *Italian:*
    - ○ *Example/enumeration:* A Bob piacciono gli sport. Ad esempio: il calcio, la gara di ostacoli e la gara di fondo.
    - ○ *Direct speech:* Lui ha detto: «Che stai facendo?»
- *Romanian:*
    - ○ *Example/enumeration:* Lui Bob îi plac sporturile. De exemplu: fotbalul, alergarea de garduri şi alergarea de fond.
    - ○ *Direct speech:* El spuse:
        — Ce faci?

Another difference is that French, Italian and Romanian use a comma to separate decimals in numbers (Ramat and Muller 2009: 79; Stan 2015: 92). Italian uses a period to separate every three digits (Serianni et al. 2017: 157); Romanian uses generally a period or a space, while French uses only a space (Ramat and Muller 2009: 79). American English generally uses a period to separate decimals and a comma to separate the thousands (Quirk et al. 2005: 394, 397).

Examples (4):
- *American English:* 8,791,123.55
- *French:* 8 791 123,55
- *Italian:* 8.791.123,55
- *Romanian:* 8.791.123,55 or 8 791 123,55

3.3. The Dash (—)

As stated in the **3.1. Quotation Marks** subsection, French and Romanian use the dash also to indicate dialogue, while American English uses quotation marks for that. There are other American English uses for the dash instead of different punctuation signs used in French, Italian, and Romanian, such as (Note: there are no spaces before or after the dash in AmE):

parentheses,

Examples (5):

- *American English:* "Other diseases common in old age—cancer, stroke, and heart disease—may lead to more severe consequences in a person with Alzheimer's disease." (Sims 2002: 140).

- *French:* « Autres maladies communes à la vieillesse (le cancer, l'accident vasculaire cérébral et des maladies cardio-vasculaires) pourraient conduire à des conséquences plus graves dans le cas d'une personne avec la maladie d'Alzheimer. »

- *Italian:* «Altre malattie comuni nella vecchiaia (cancro, ictus e malattie cardiache) possono portare a conseguenze più gravi in una persona con malattia di Alzheimer.»

- *Romanian:* „Alte boli obișnuite pentru vârsta a treia (cancer, accident vascular cerebral și boală cardiovasculară) pot duce la consecințe mai grave, la o persoană cu boala Alzheimer."

commas,

Examples (6):

- *American English:* The two substances are bactericidal—that is, they kill bacteria.
- *French:* Les deux substances sont bactéricides, c'est-à-dire, elles détruisent les bactéries.
- *Italian:* Le due sostanze sono battericide, cioè uccidono i batteri.
- *Romanian:* Cele două substanţe sunt bactericide, adică distrug bacteriile.

colon,

Examples (7):

- *American English:* "This treatment is for smaller abscesses in relatively less dangerous areas of the body—limbs, trunk, back of the neck." (Polsdorfer 2002: 14)
- *French:* « Ce traitement est pour des abcès plus petits, dans des zones relativement moins dangereuses du corps : les membres, le tronc, la nuque. »
- *Italian:* «Questo trattamento è indicato per ascessi più piccoli in zone relativamente meno pericolose delle aree del corpo: gli arti, il tronco, la nuca.»
- *Romanian:* „Acest tratament este pentru abcese mai mici, în zone relativ mai puţin periculoase ale corpului: membre, trunchi, ceafă."

ellipsis,

Examples (8):

- *American English:* "In five years of basketball, I didn't—" He stopped in mid-sentence.

- *French:* « En cinq ans de basket-ball, je n'ai… » Il s'arrêta au milieu de sa phrase.
- *Italian:* — In cinque anni di pallacanestro, io non ho… — si fermò a metà frase.
- *Romanian:* — În cinci ani de baschet, n-am…, și-a întrerupt el brusc vorbirea.

The ellipsis is also used as an interruption in a quote, to mark a fragment is missing from a citation. French, Italian, and Romanian put it in brackets – round for French (Riegel et al. 2015: 159), and square for Italian (Mortara Garavelli 2003: 113) and Romanian (Stan 2015: 64; Popa and Popa 2015: 451). American English does not (Quirk et al. 2005: 1636).

Examples (9):
- *American English:* "Ipratropium bromide … and atropine sulfate are anticholinergic drugs used for the treatment of asthma." (Robinson and Granger 2002: 120)
- *French:* « Le bromure d'ipratropium (…) et l'atropine sulfate sont des médicaments anticholinergiques utilisés pour le traitement de l'asthme. »
- *Italian:* «L'ipratropio bromuro [...] e l'atropina solfato sono farmaci anticolinergici utilizzati per il trattamento dell'asma.»
- *Romanian:* „Bromura de ipratropiu […] și sulfatul de atropină sunt medicamente anticolinergice folosite pentru tratarea astmei."

4. Results and discussion

4.1. Results

Before getting to the actual results, it must be said that the three bilingual corpora are not equal in size (they do not contain the same amount of data): the French/English corpus is the largest at 6.85 GB unarchived (the English file has 3.16 GB and the French one, 3.68 GB), the Romanian/English corpus is the smallest at 370 MB unarchived (181 MB the English file; 189 MB the Romanian file), and the Italian/English corpus has 1.79 GB unarchived (887 MB the English file; 952 MB the Italian file). For that reason, the author has considered percentages to be more relevant than the actual number of instances encountered in a search.

To open files of this size the author has used the free software *glogg* (Bonnefon 2017), a multi-platform application created for browsing and searching through long or complex log files. The software allows the use of regular expressions (a sequence of characters defining a search pattern), presenting a results window, which, together with complex regular expressions, allows easy isolation of the meaningful lines in the file.

4.1.1. French / English

Quotation marks

A search of the English file of the French / English bilingual corpus shows that there are 1,026,656 instances of double inverted commas in the English file (there could be also quotation within quotations included in this result, but the author could not find a way to isolate them). Another search revealed 52,015 instances of guillemets («

»). If the double inverted commas result is added to the guillemets result, one gets a total number of 1,078,671 instances of quotation marks, out of which the guillemets represent **4.82%**.

The Comma

Example/enumeration

In this case, simply searching for a comma would have led to nowhere, as the American English style of using the comma does not really stand out (i.e., it is not that different than the way the other languages use it). The author thought that a more useful search would be that of the French style of using punctuation in general, and in this particular case the colon, which is adding a space in front of it (as explained in the **Introduction** and in the third section, **Punctuation as used in American English, French, Italian, and Romanian**). Thus, this search of the English file revealed 313,202 instances where a space is put in front of the colon (" : ").

Another search revealed a total of 1,059,299 instances of a colon being used – but the search counted also expressions of time (e.g. "12:05 PM", etc.). The author tried to correct that by searching for the number of times this kind of expressions are used, using the regular expression "[0-9]:[0-9]" (without the quotation marks). This means searching for a number containing any number of digits, followed by a colon, followed by any number of digits (this regular expression or a variation of it has been used throughout this study). The last search resulted in 617,964 matches. After subtracting the number of expressions of time from the total number of colon uses, one gets a final result of 441,335 instances where a colon was used in the English corpus. This is not perfect, but it's the closest to an exact result that the author could get.

In the end, the French style represented **70.97%** out of all the final uses of a colon in the English file.

Direct speech

A search for the French style of marking direct speech (a space before the colon and after the guillemet - " : « " – without the inverted commas) gave 916 total results (with and without the space after the guillemet).

The search for the American English style (a comma then inverted commas – ", "") resulted in 60,277 matches.

The total number of instances of a direct speech marker used in the English file of the French/English corpus was 916 + 60,277 = 61,193, out of which the French style represented **1.50%**.

Numbers

The first two searches of the English file aimed to find the American English usages of the punctuation when it comes to numbers. One search (using the regular expression " [0-9].[0-9] ") revealed 121,716 instances where a period was used to separate the decimals – although, unfortunately, the search counted also numbered lists (e.g. "table 3.5", etc.), while another search (" [0-9],[0-9].[0-9] ") resulted in 65,529 instances of a comma separating the thousands.

Another two searches found 10,361 instances of a comma separating the decimals (" [0-9],[0-9] "), and 282,609 instances of a space separating the thousands ("[0-9] [0-9]"), but the latter counted also telephone numbers. Trying to counter that, another search was made ("+[0-9] [0-9]"), counting the telephone numbers (most of them had an international prefix), which resulted in 179 instances. When the telephone number result is subtracted from the space-separated thousands result we have 282,430 instances of a space separating the thousands.

If the period-separated decimals are added to the comma-separated ones, one gets a result of 132,077 instances of decimals separated from the integers – out of which the French style represents ±7.84% (taking into account a certain margin of error created by the extra count). When the comma-separated thousands are added to the "final" result of the space-separated thousands, one gets 347,959 types of separation of the thousands, out of which the French style represents ±81.17% (taking into account the same margin of error).

The Dash

There are 447 instances where the *dash* is used in the English file of the French / English bilingual corpus. However, the use of other punctuation marks instead of the dash in French (and the other languages) is purely contextual, and it does not stand out in any searchable way (at least not with *glogg*) – as opposed to, for instance, the guillemets, or the colon with a space in front of it. Due to the sheer number of results, it would be impossible to tell which uses are American English and which are French.

The only searchable item in this section would be the different way in which the four languages mark a missing fragment from a text – i.e., the *ellipsis*. Thus, in the English file of the French/English corpus there were 32,894 matches for the French style ("**(...)**"). Another search revealed 38,497 instances where the ellipsis was used according to the AmE norm – a space before and after it (" **...** "). An addition of the two results gives us a total of 71,391 uses of an ellipsis to mark a missing fragment, of which the French style represents **46.07%**.

4.1.2. Italian / English

Quotation marks

In regard to the Italian/English corpus, a search revealed that there are 359,417 instances of quotation marks in English (adding the double inverted commas to the guillemets), of which 20,542 instances of guillemets (« »), representing **5.71%**.

The Comma

In the case of a comma or colon used in *examples/enumerations*, it would be irrelevant to search the corpus, because neither is used in any stand-out manner, like in French. It would stand out only if their use is regarded in context, which the size of the corpus makes almost impossible.

Direct speech

In this case, a search (": «") of the English file revealed 4,044 instances where guillemets are used after a colon.

The search for American English style of marking direct speech (", "") resulted in 19,511 matches, but it included also enumerations of words in quotes (e.g., 162 "standard", "lateral sea view" rooms, etc.). Unfortunately, this extra count cannot be rectified. If one does decide to add both results of direct speech markers, one would get a total of 23,555, out of which the Italian style would represent ±**17.17%**. The actual percentage is probably higher, considering that the real number of AmE type of direct speech markers is lower than what the search showed.

Numbers

Two searches of the English file revealed 56,902 instances where a period was used to separate the decimals (" [0-9].[0-9] ") and 15,102 instances of a comma separating the thousands (" [0-9],[0-9].[0-9] "), the latter, however, comprising also enumerations (e.g. "4, 5, 6") and instances of numbers with a comma next to them (e.g. "1932, …", etc.).

A third search (" [0-9],[0-9] ") revealed 8,883 instances where a comma was used to separate the decimals. A fourth search (" [0-9].[0-9],[0-9] ") concerning instances where a period is used to separate the thousands gave only one match, which was an enumeration ("subway lines 1.2,3…"), thus nullifying the result.

The addition of the AmE style of separating the decimals and the Italian style leads to a total result of 65,785 instances, of which the Italian style represents **13.5%**.

The Dash

The English file of the Italian/English corpus contains 44 uses of the dash, all of which seem to be in accordance with the AmE usage. But when it comes to the other punctuation marks that are used in the other three languages instead of the dash, there is the same problem encountered and explained in the same subsection of the

French/English corpus – that the understanding of that usage is contextual, thus making a search irrelevant (in the sense that it would result in a multitude of matches that would be impossible to check as they have no stand-out quality).

As in the case of the previous corpus (French/English), the only punctuation mark that can be searched successfully is the *ellipsis*, the way it is used in Italian to mark missing fragments in a text ("**[...]**"). As far as it is concerned, there were 112 instances found in the English file of the Italian/English corpus. Another search resulted in 22,307 instances where the ellipsis was used to mark missing fragments in the style of American English (" ... "). An addition of the two results gives us the sum of 22,419, out of which the Italian style represents **0.5%**.

4.1.3. Romanian / English
Quotation marks

The Romanian/English corpus contains 23,791 instances of quotation marks (counting double inverted commas, guillemets and curved quotation marks) in English, of which 902 instances of curved quotation marks („") and 416 instances of guillemets. The total number of Romanian style quotation marks is 902 + 416 = 1,318, which represents **5.54%**.

The Comma

Example/enumeration

Here one encounters the same problem as in the same subsection of the Italian/English corpus analysis. The use of commas and/or colons is relevant only in context (not being used in any manner that stands out), thus making a search useless.

Direct speech

The search produced 1,039 matches for the AmE style (", ""), but the search also included words in quotes (e.g. 'At present, "IEZERESS" products...' etc.). The Romanian style (": —") had only 5 matches, of which only one is direct speech, the rest are parts of lists. That particular instance can be considered a mistake.

Numbers

The first two searches of the English file revealed 2,189 instances where a period was used to separate the decimals (" [0-9].[0-9] ") and 850 instances of a comma separating the thousands (" [0-9],[0-9].[0-9] "), but the latter comprises also instances of numbers with a comma next to them (e.g. "2008, ...").

A third search (" [0-9],[0-9] ") revealed 157 instances where a comma was used to separate the decimals, but it counted also enumerations (e.g. "0, 2, 3, ...", etc.). A fourth search ("[0-9] [0-9]") revealed 261,464 instances of a space separating the thousands, however this included also just numbers with a space between them (e.g. "vol. 186 2013", etc.). A fifth search (" [0-9].[0-9],[0-9] ") concerning instances where a period is used to separate the thousands gave 244 matches, but none of them were about period-separated thousands, thus rendering the search irrelevant.

By adding the period-separated decimals with the comma-separated ones, we get a sum of 2,346 total uses of punctuation to separate the decimals, out of which the Romanian style represents ±**6.69%** (taking again into account a certain margin of error created by the extra count). The addition of the comma-separated thousands and the space-separated ones gives the result of 262,314 total uses of punctuation to separate the thousands, out of which the Romanian style use represents ±**99.67%** (although, again, one must take into account the same margin of error).

The Dash

The search revealed only two uses of the dash in the English file of the Romanian/English corpus, both of which are in accordance with the common American English usage. The same problem was encountered here, as in the case of the same subsection of the other two corpora analyses. Just like in the previous cases, the only relevant search was for the Romanian use of *ellipsis* as a marker for missing text ("**[...]**"). The search returned no results regarding such uses.

Table 1 – Centralized Results

	French/ English		Italian/ English		Romanian/ English	
Quotation marks	4.82%		5.71%		5.54%	
Example/enumera tion punctuation markers	70.97%		-		-	
Direct speech punctuation markers	1.50%		17.17%		-	
Punctuation used in numbers	decima ls	thousan ds	decima ls	thousan ds	decima ls	thousan ds
	7.84%	81.17%	13.5%	-	6.69%	99.67%
Ellipsis (marking missing text)	46.07%		0.5%		-	

4.2. Discussion

As mentioned in the **Introduction**, the corpora used for this study contain texts "to/from English" (Koehn et al. 2018); due to the large amount of data (especially in the case of the French/English corpus), it was impossible to tell which parts were original and which were translated. Another problem was the indiscriminate indexation of all "English" texts, as stated also in the **Introduction**, without any distinction between the variations of English and French. When it comes to multilingual researches of this type, there is a general issue with many corpora, in the sense that they are not specific enough, or particularized enough, or clear enough about their content (i.e., which is original, which is translation). A third problem were the author's admitted limited skills as a coder. Maybe if he was better at creating or adapting regular expressions, or if he would have used a different application, the results would have been more relevant, in the sense that it would have revealed, perhaps, more about the linguistic errors in the corpora.

That being said, the results (centralized in table 1) are worth discussing. The very low percentages can be viewed as linguistic mistakes, while the high ones, as errors. However, the author thinks the percentage of guillemets in the English files of the French/English and Italian/English corpora, although low, can be important for an authorship analysis, especially because American English does not use them.

In the French/English corpus, the French style of a space around the colon is used too much to be a mistake – it can only be a linguistic error. As far as the example/enumeration punctuation markers are concerned (in the French/English corpus), or the markers for thousands (in the French/English and Romanian/English corpora, but **not** in the Italian corpus), or even the ellipsis (in the same French/English corpus), even taking into consideration a margin of error (explained in their subsections), the percentages are still very high to be just mistakes, and can be considered covert errors. Overall, the French/English corpus produced the most results because of the French language's particular use of punctuation.

5. Conclusions

The questions of how and if French, Italian, and Romanian uses of punctuation can be identified in American English have been answered, albeit partially and with certain caveats. By searching through multilingual corpora, basing the search on pre-established rules that were observed and described by linguists in descriptive grammars, such uses were identified, with some percentages being surprisingly high, revealing several cases of covert linguistic errors.

One of the several problems (most of them addressed in the **4.2. Discussion** subsection), however, is that the identification of native speaker authors through punctuation is itself in its infancy, and therefore extrapolating this to non-native author analysis is problematic. Nevertheless, despite these reservations, this study could be considered a preliminary to further investigation and is the first time, to the author's knowledge, that this question has been broached in research.

6. References

1. Bonnefon, N. (2017) *glogg*. http://glogg.bonnefon.org. Accessed 26 June 2019.

2. Chaski, C.E. (2001) Empirical evaluations of language-based author identification techniques. *Forensic Linguistics* 8(1): 1-65. doi: 10.1558/ijsll.v8i1.1.

3. Chaski, C.E. (2005) Who's At The Keyboard? Authorship Attribution in Digital Evidence Investigations. *International Journal of Digital Evidence* 4(1): 1-13.

4. Chaski, C.E. (2007) The Keyboard Dilemma and Authorship Identification. International Federation for Information Processing Digital Library, *Advances in Digital Forensics III*: 59-71. doi: 10.1007/978-0-387-73742-3_9.

5. Chaski, C.E. (2012) Author Identification in the Forensic Setting. In P.M. Tiersma and L.M. Solan (eds.) *The Oxford Handbook of Language and Law* 489-503. Oxford: Oxford University Press.

6. Choi, D. (2002) Style and Stylistics of Korean Writing. In G.R. McMenamin, *Forensic Linguistics: Advances in Forensic Stylistics* 279-294. CRC Press.

7. Corder, S.P. (1967) The significance of learners' errors. *International Review of Applied Linguistics*, 5: 161–170.

8. Coulthard, M. and Johnson, A. (2007) *An introduction to forensic linguistics: language in evidence*. London: Routledge.

9. Coulthard, M. (2013) On admissible linguistic evidence. *Journal of Law and Policy*, 21 (2): 441-466.

10. Coulthard, M.; Johnson, A.; Kredens, K. and Woolls, D. (2013) Plagiarism: Four forensic linguists' responses to suspected plagiarism. In Coulthard, M. and Johnson, A. (eds.), *The Routledge Handbook of Forensic Linguistics* 523-538. London: Routledge.

11. Eades, D. (2013) Nationality claims: language analysis and asylum cases. In M. Coulthard and A. Johnson (eds.) *The Routledge Handbook of Forensic Linguistics* 411-507. London: Routledge

12. Eagleson, R. D. (1990) Linguist for the Prosecution. *Sydney Studies in Society and Culture*, 6.

13. Ellis, R. (1994) *The Study of Second Language Acquisition*. Oxford: Oxford University Press

14. Gass, S.M. and Selinker, L. (2008) *Second Language Acquisition: An Introductory Course. Third edition.* London: Routledge.

15. Grant, T. and Baker, K. (2001) Identifying reliable, valid markers of authorship: a response to Chaski. *Forensic Linguistics* 8(1): 66-79.

16. Harris, S.S. (2005) Anemia. In D. Levinson and K. Christensen (eds.) *The Berkshire Encyclopedia of World Sport, vol. 1*, 57. Berkshire Publishing Group LLC.

17. Ishihara, S. (2017) Strength of forensic text comparison evidence from stylometric features: a multivariate likelihood ratio-based analysis. *The International Journal of Speech, Language and the Law* 24(1): 67-98. doi:10.1558/ijsll.30305.

18. Koehn, P.; Heafield, K.; Forcada, M.L.; et al. (2018) *ParaCrawl Corpus version 1.0.* LINDAT/CLARIN digital library at the Institute of Formal and Applied Linguistics (ÚFAL), Faculty of

Mathematics and Physics, Charles University, http://hdl.handle.net/11372/LRT-2610. Accessed 24 June 2019.

19. Lupescu, L. (2016) American English, French, and Romanian: Punctuation Differences. *Translation Journal*, October 2016. https://translationjournal.net/October-2016/american-english-french-and-romanian-punctuation-differences.html. Accessed 24 June 2019.

20. McMenamin, G.R. (2001) Style markers in authorship studies. *Forensic Linguistics* 8(2): 93-97.

21. McMenamin, G.R. (2002) *Forensic Linguistics: Advances in Forensic Stylistics*. CRC Press.

22. McMenamin, G.R. (2013) Forensic stylistics: Theory and practice of forensic stylistics. In M. Coulthard and A. Johnson (eds.) *The Routledge Handbook of Forensic Linguistics* 487-507. London: Routledge

23. Michell, C.S. (2013) *Investigating the Use of Forensic Stylistic and Stylometric Techniques in the Analyses of Authorship on A Publicly Accessible Social Networking Site (Facebook)*. Master's dissertation, University of South Africa, unpublished.

24. Mistry, P.J. (2002) Stylistic Features of Gujarati Letter Writing: A Note. In G.R. McMenamin, *Forensic Linguistics: Advances in Forensic Stylistics* 269-278. CRC Press.

25. Mortara Garavelli, B. (2003) *Prontuario di punteggiatura*. Bari: Editori Laterza.

26. Narayanan, A.; Paskov, H.; Gong, N.Z.; Bethencourt, J.; Stefanov, E.; Shin, E.C.R.; Song, D. (2012) On the Feasibility of

Internet-Scale Author Identification. In *2012 IEEE Symposium on Security and Privacy*: 300-314. IEEE.

27. Olsson, J. (2013) *Wordcrime: Solving Crime through Forensic Linguistics*. Reprint. London: Bloomsbury Academic.

28. Patrick, P.L. (2012) Language analysis for determination of origin: objective evidence for refugee status determination. In P.M. Tiersma and L.M. Solan (eds.) *The Oxford Handbook of Language and Law* 533-546. Oxford: Oxford University Press.

29. Perkins, R. and Grant, T. (2018) Native language influence detection for forensic authorship analysis: Identifying L1 Persian bloggers. *The International Journal of Speech, Language and the Law* 25(1): 1-20. https://doi:10.1558/ijsll.30844

30. Pestian, J., Nasrallah, H., Matykiewicz, P., Bennett, A., Leenaars, A. (2010) Suicide Note Classification Using Natural Language Processing: A Content Analysis. *Biomedical Informatics Insights* 3: 19–28.

31. Polsdorfer, J.R. (2002) Abscess. In J.L. Longe and D.S. Blanchfield (eds.) *The Gale Encyclopedia of Medicine, Second Edition, vol. 1*, 14. Gale Group.

32. Popa, I. and Popa, M. (2015) *Limba română: gramatică, fonetică, vocabular, ortografie și ortoepie. Ed. a 2-a, rev. în conformitate cu noul DOOM.* Bucharest: NICULESCU.

33. Prokofyeva, T. (2013) *Language Use in Two Types of Suicide Texts.* Master's dissertation, Linköping University (Sweden), unpublished.

34. Quirk, R., Greenbaum, S., Leech, G. and Svartvik, J. (2005) *A Comprehensive Grammar of the English Language.* Longman

35. Ramat, A., and Muller, R. (2009) *Le Ramat européen de la typographie.* Dijon: Editions De Champlain.

36. Rico-Sulayes, A. (2011) Statistical authorship attribution of Mexican drug trafficking online forum posts. *The International Journal of Speech, Language and the Law* 18(1): 53-74. doi:10.1558/ijsll.v18i1.53.

37. Riegel, M., Pellat, J.-C., and Rioul, R. (2015) *Grammaire méthodique du français. 5ᵉ édition, 2ᵉ tirage.* Paris: Presses Universitaires de France.

38. Robinson, R. and Granger, J. (2002) Allergies. In J.L. Longe and D.S. Blanchfield (eds.) *The Gale Encyclopedia of Medicine, Second Edition, vol. 1,* 120. Gale Group.

39. Saint-Exupéry, A. de (2015a) (1943) *The Little Prince.* English translation: Gregory Norminton. Alma Classics Ltd.

40. Saint-Exupéry, A. de (2015b) (1943) *Micul prinţ.* Romanian translation: Lucian Pricop. Bucharest: Cartex.

41. Saint-Exupéry, A. de (2016a) (1943) *Le Petit Prince.* Paris: Gallimard.

42. Saint-Exupéry, A. de (2016b) (1943) *Il Piccolo Principe.* Italian translation: Franco Perini. Liberi Pomi (ePub edition)

43. Serianni, L., Castelvecchi, A., and Patota, G. (2017) (1997) *Italiano.* Milano: Garzanti.

44. Sims, J. (2002) Alzheimer's disease. In J.L. Longe and D.S. Blanchfield (eds.) *The Gale Encyclopedia of Medicine, Second Edition, vol. 1,* 140. Gale Group.

45. Solan, L. M. (2013) Intuition versus algorithm: The case of forensic authorship attribution. *JL & Pol'y* 21: 551-576.

46. Sousa-Silva, R. (2014) Detecting translingual plagiarism and the backlash against translation plagiarists. *Language and Law / Linguagem e Direito* 1(1): 70-94.

47. Stan, M. (2015) *Ghid ortografic, ortoepic și de punctuație.* Bucharest: ART.

48. Tetreault, J., Blanchard, D., Cahill, A., Chodorow, M. (2012) Native Tongues, Lost and Found: Resources and Empirical Evaluations in Native Language Identification. *Proceedings of COLING 2012: Technical Papers.* 2585–2602. Mumbai.

49. Trask, R.L. (1997) *The Penguin Guide to Punctuation.* London: Penguin.

50. Woolls, D. (2013) Computational forensic linguistics: searching for similarity in large specialised corpora. In M. Coulthard and A. Johnson (eds.) *The Routledge Handbook of Forensic Linguistics* 576-590. London: Routledge.

51. Yasuda, W. (2002) Style and Stylistics of Japanese. In G.R. McMenamin, *Forensic Linguistics: Advances in Forensic Stylistics* 295-311. CRC Press.

Made in the USA
Monee, IL
04 March 2021

61891434R10059